REPAIR OF THE SOUL

RELATIONAL PERSPECTIVES BOOK SERIES

Volume 38

LEWIS ARON AND ADRIENNE HARRIS
SERIES EDITORS

Rita Wiley McCleary
Conversing with Uncertainty:
Practicing Psychotherapy in a Hospital Setting

Charles Spezzano
Affect in Psychoanalysis: A Clinical Synthesis

Neil Altman
The Analyst in the Inner City: Race, Class, and Culture
through a Psychoanalytic Lens

Lewis Aron
A Meeting of Minds: Mutuality in Psychoanalysis

Joyce A. Slochower
Holding and Psychoanalysis: A Relational Perspective

Barbara Gerson, editor
The Therapist as a Person: Life Crises, Life Choices,
Life Experiences, and Their Effects on Treatment

Charles Spezzano and Gerald J. Gargiulo, editors
Soul on the Couch: Spirituality, Religion, and Morality
in Contemporary Psychoanalysis

Donnel B. Stern
Unformulated Experience: From Dissociation
to Imagination in Psychoanalysis

Stephen A. Mitchell
Influence and Autonomy in Psychoanalysis
Neil J. Skolnick and David E. Scharff, editors
Fairbairn, Then and Now

Stuart A. Pizer
Building Bridges: Negotiation of
Paradox in Psychoanalysis

Lewis Aron and Frances Sommer Anderson, editors
Relational Perspectives on the Body

Karen Maroda
Seduction, Surrender, and Transformation:
Emotional Engagement in the Analytic Process

Stephen A. Mitchell and Lewis Aron, editors
Relational Psychoanalysis:
The Emergence of a Tradition

Rochelle G. K. Kainer
The Collapse of the Self and Its Therapeutic Restoration

Kenneth A. Frank
Psychoanalytic Participation:
Action, Interaction, and Integration

Sue Grand
The Reproduction of Evil:
A Clinical and Cultural Perspective

Steven H. Cooper
Objects of Hope: Exploring Possibility
and Limit in Psychoanalysis

James S. Grotstein
Who Is the Dreamer, Who Dreams the Dream?
A Study of Psychic Presences

Stephen A. Mitchell
Relationality: From Attachment to Intersubjectivity

Peter G. M. Carnochan
Looking for Ground: Countertransference and
the Problem of Value in Psychoanalysis

Muriel Dimen
Sexuality, Intimacy, Power

Susan W. Coates, Jane L. Rosenthal, and
Daniel S. Schechter, editors
September 11: Trauma and Human Bonds

Randall Lehman Sorenson
Minding Spirituality

Adrienne Harris
Gender as Soft Assembly

Emanuel Berman
Impossible Training: A Relational View
of Psychoanalytic Education

Carlo Strenger
The Designed Self: Psychoanalysis
and Contemporary Identities

Lewis Aron and Adrienne Harris, editors
Relational Psychoanalysis, V. II:
Innovation and Expansion

Sebastiano Santostefano
Child Therapy in the Great Outdoors:
A Relational View

James T. McLaughlin
The Healer's Bent: Solitude and Dialogue
in the Clinical Encounter

Danielle Knafo and Kenneth Feiner
Unconscious Fantasies and the Relational World

Sheldon Bach
Getting from Here to There:
Analytic Love, Analytic Process

Katie Gentile
Creating Bodies: Eating Disorders
as Self-Destructive Survival

Melanie Suchet, Adrienne Harris, and
Lewis Aron, editors
Relational Psychoanalysis, V. III: New Voices

Brent Willock
Comparative-Integrative Psychoanalysis: A Relational
Perspective for the Discipline's Second Century

Frances Sommer Anderson, editor
Bodies in Treatment: The Unspoken Dimension

Deborah Browning, editor
Adolescent Identities: A Collection of Readings

Karen E. Starr
Repair of the Soul: Metaphors of Transformation
in Jewish Mysticism and Psychoanalysis

REPAIR OF THE SOUL

METAPHORS OF TRANSFORMATION IN JEWISH MYSTICISM AND PSYCHOANALYSIS

KAREN E. STARR

FOREWORD BY LEWIS ARON

Routledge
Taylor & Francis Group
New York   London

Cover art: *Jacob's Ladder* (© 1997) by Michael Bogdanow (www.MichaelBogdanow.com). Inspired by Jacob's dream from Genesis 28:10-19, "a ladder was set up on the earth, its top reaching the heavens... messengers of God were going up and down on it," it is part of the artist's "Visions of Torah" series of contemporary, spiritual paintings and reproductions inspired by Judaic texts.

Routledge   Routledge
Taylor & Francis Group   Taylor & Francis Group
270 Madison Avenue   27 Church Road
New York, NY 10016   Hove, East Sussex BN3 2FA

© 2008 by Taylor & Francis Group, LLC

Printed in the United States of America on acid-free paper
10 9 8 7 6 5 4 3 2 1

International Standard Book Number-13: 978-0-88163-487-7 (Softcover) 978-0-88163-486-0 (0)

Library of Congress Cataloging-in-Publication Data

Starr, Karen E.
    Repair of the soul: metaphors of transformation in Jewish mysticism and pyschoanalysis / Karen E. Starr.
        p. cm. -- (Relational perspectives ; 38)
    Includes bibliographical references and index.
    ISBN 978-0-88163-487-7 (alk. paper) -- ISBN 978-0-88163-486-0 (alk. paper) 1.
    Judaism and psychoanalysis. 2. Mysticism--Judaism. 3. Cabala. I. Title.

BM538.P68S73 2008
296.3'71--dc22   2008013086

Visit the Taylor & Francis Web site at
http://www.taylorandfrancis.com

and the Routledge Web site at
http://www.routledgementalhealth.com

In memory of my parents,
Bertha and Siegfried Horowitz

Contents

Foreword ix

Preface xix

Acknowledgments xxiii

1. Introduction: The Kabbalah 1

2. Psychoanalysis and the Kabbalah: A Case for Dialogue 9

3. Transformation 21

4. The Interpretive Encounter 45

5. Faith as the Fulcrum of Psychic Change 63

6. The Transformation of Evil 87

Epilogue: Jacob's Ladder 113

References 119

Index 127

Foreword

"Also from Above Will Come Help"

Lewis Aron

 "Also from above will come help." A strong voice from the Heavens called out just when I felt a desperate need and under special, magical, emotionally loaded, transitional, luminal, even Holy circumstances. Not imaginary, not just in my head, but a real voice, a strong but distant voice. But I did not believe in heavenly voices and so felt stunned, confused, for a split second even transported beside myself, outside of myself, dissociated, split, transported, and transformed at least momentarily, just for a second, but in a way that I have never forgotten, even now, almost four decades later.

It was 1970 and I was a boy of 17 living, and as we would say, "learning" for a semester in a yeshiva in Israel. It was our last night of the semester and we—my friends, dorm mates, all young men—were to fly home the following morning. We must have been busy packing and saying our goodbyes, preparing to leave what had been a remarkable few months. Many of us were deeply ambivalent about returning home, "descending" from the Holy land. Some in fact stayed on to "learn" in yeshiva for several more years, as I planned to do. Some remained to join the Israeli army. And some were returning to begin college.

By now it was late in the evening, probably later than it should have been when we realized it was time for evening prayers. We decided that rather than pray at the school we would walk to the Western Wall in the Old City. It wasn't a far walk from our school in Rechavia and we had all walked there many times. In fact, every Friday evening we would walk with groups of other yeshiva students, marching, almost dancing together to the Wall to say our prayers, welcoming the Sabbath. Walking together in our open-collared white shirts, we sang and chanted religious hymns, to pray on Friday nights at the Holiest site of Judaism, and we joined together. It was exhilarating, moving, and inspirational; a group experience, a spiritual and yet bodily activity powerful enough to last a lifetime. So we all knew the way through the Old City, even some of the shortcuts.

In 1970, we could walk through the Old City even at night without fear. In those days, not long after the Six-Day War, Jews were heady with victory and full of pride. There was hope for a lasting peace and the markets of the Old City were busy with business and shopping, filled with tourists, and seemed safe. And so off we went in the dark through the Old City, through the Jewish Quarter and to the Wall. Only just recently, following Israel's victory during the 1967 Six-Day War, had the Western Wall come under Israeli control.

It was a beautiful night and we were all in good spirits, but our mood was bittersweet. We were feeling mournful about the end of our stay and ambivalent about our return to parents and home and whatever would come next. We were all struck by just how quiet it was at the Wall. The Wall was always busy with visitors, tourists, guides, families, students, soldiers, people taking photos, saying their prayers, or placing slips of paper with prayers into the cracks of the Wall. But this was late on a June evening and we were surprised to find it silent, with very few people there.

Jewish sources, including the Zohar, the Holy foundational text of the Kabbalah, suggest that the Divine Presence rests on the Western Wall. It is told that great Jewish sages, including Isaac Luria, the famous 16th-century mystic of Safed, experienced revelations of the Divine Presence at the Wall. The Wall itself, The *Kotel,* is a remnant of the Second Temple, which was built on the foundations of the destroyed First Temple, thought to have been built by King David. Sometimes known as the "Wailing Wall" because it is where Jews have historically wept for the lost Temple, it is adjacent to the Temple Mount, the Holiest site of Judaism. None of us had ever actually gone up to see the Temple Mount area as it is forbidden by Jewish law to set foot on such Holy space. It was the site of the Holy of Holies, the innermost sanctum of the Temple where only the High Priest, the priest of priests would set foot, and then only on the Holiest of Holy Days, and even then, even he was at risk for his life to enter such a Holy space. This was the very spot, the very rock on which Abraham prepared to sacrifice his son Isaac and where he heard a voice cry out to him.

So here we were in need of a *minyan,* by tradition and religious law a quorum of ten men, the minimum number needed for public prayer. We asked whatever other men were there to join us but there were only nine of us altogether at the Wall that night. And so we waited. We were sure that it would only be a matter of moments for someone to come along, just one more Jewish man to join us to constitute a quorum so that we could begin prayers; it would just take a few minutes. But on that crystal-clear night, for some strange reason that we could not fathom, no one came. We waited but began to feel rushed. We were leaving the next morning and, besides, it was late, and our dorm counselor must by now be anxious and annoyed that we had not returned. We'd have to get up early to leave for the airport. We really couldn't, shouldn't wait much longer. But we couldn't pray together without a 10th man.

I was emotional, deeply ambivalent about returning home. It had been my first extended stay away from my family and it wasn't easy for me. Yet my plan was to go home just for the summer and then to return to Israel to study in yeshiva for another year or two. I didn't know what it would be like to go home, whether I'd really want to return. Would I stay as religious as I had become? Would I be corrupted by my return to a secular world? And beneath my conscious concerns I must have been anxious about rejoining but also anxious anticipating further separations from my family, as well as moving out of an all-male environment and back to some pressure I felt about dating. Anxious about college and career choices, worried about my temptations to rejoin my friends experimenting with drugs; it was after all 1970 and I was 17. I was still three years away from beginning my own personal analysis; it might as well have been eons. But now we were late and needed a 10th man.

"*Gam me'lemalah yazor*" "Also from above will come help." We all heard this voice. I knew it wasn't just me, because we all looked up, each stunned. A strong voice, a man's voice, loud and clear but very far away. And then silence for a brief moment. We looked up but there was nothing and no one. The voice seemed to come from the night sky, way up above us, but there was nothing up there. We glanced at each other, was it a mistake, an illusion? And then a second time. The same words in the same certain tone. "*Gam me'lemalah yazor*" "Also from above will come help." This time I was shaken. Absolutely beside myself. There was not enough time for me to actually process my thoughts; it was much too quick for that. But I have no doubt, and have never doubted in all of these years since, that for at least one moment in my life I was certain that I had heard a Heavenly Voice, a "*Bat-Kol.*" Was it miraculous? Would God Himself help us constitute a *minyan*? Had God sent an angel, a Heavenly agent to join us on this night?

I had been raised in a modern Orthodox home and community. We were not taught to expect voices from the Heavens. The Rabbinic tradition had been very conservative about direct communications from God. Rabbinic Judaism developed at a time of religious and political upheaval. Within the span of about a century, the Jews had to cope with the loss of political sovereignty, a series of military defeats, the loss of their capital and their homeland, the destruction of the Temple, and the rise of Christianity and Gnosticism, as well as the crisis of faith initiated by all of these catastrophes. In the biblical era, God's law had been mediated by prophets and oracular devices that were assumed to provide unambiguous signs. For the rabbis, prophecy was exceedingly dangerous. Who, after all, could be certain of who was a true prophet? And, furthermore, if one were to follow prophets—or, more accurately, if the entire community were to follow a prophet—then the law could be subject to change or abrogation at any time and hence prophecy could lead to radical change and legal chaos. The rabbis argued that after the destruction of the first temple, God's will was no longer made known through prophecy. Instead, the rabbis claimed, God's will was determined through their interpretation of God's Torah. Because the text was ambiguous and interpretations were often contradictory and incompatible, they developed a legal system based on majority rule. They then took the authority that had been vested in the prophets and judges and claimed it for rabbinic interpretation. They discouraged attending to direct Divine communication because they anticipated that these mystical experiences would destabilize normative legal authority. Heavenly voices were suspect. Mysticism was always potentially antinomian.

So I was not raised to expect to hear Heavenly voices. I repeatedly heard as a child that when you pray, you speak to God, but when you learn, God speaks to you. Learning, a passionate, engaged, spiritual activity, the deep study of texts, was as close as I ever expected to come to hearing God's voice.

There were some lights shining on the Wall, it was not completely dark, and the lights may have made it harder for us to see. But we soon recognized that the voice was that of an Israeli soldier who was stationed way up on the Temple Mount as a guard. It was this soldier who must have been paying attention down below to a group of boys looking for a tenth to pray. He was offering to have us count him in. It turned out that our Heavenly Voice was in fact a young soldier, Uzi in hand, ready as he stood guard this night, to be counted for a *minyan*. Later we learned his name. He called himself Eli.[1]

Truly, to my astonishment, and quite literally, I lived the realization of the words of the 11th-century Jewish mystical poet Yehuda Halevi, "Going out to meet You, I found You coming toward me" (quoted in Ostow, 2007, p. 57).

* * * * * * * *

It is a pleasure and a privilege for me to write this Foreword to Karen Starr's *Repair of the Soul: Metaphors of Transformation in Jewish Mysticism and Psychoanalysis*. Karen has written a beautiful and scholarly exegesis, examining several important themes that overlap psychoanalysis and the Jewish mystical tradition. Perhaps it makes sense to begin this study with the recognition that both psychoanalysis and the mainstream Rabbinic Jewish tradition were rationalistic traditions; both were deeply skeptical of irrationality and mysticism (see Aron, 2004).

Nevertheless, the bifurcation of normative religion with Kabbalah and the Jewish mystical tradition has been overstated. Back in the 1970s, Abraham Heschel disagreed with the then dominant modern scholar of Jewish mysticism, Gershom Scholem, who emphasized the antinomian nature of Jewish mysticism. That is, Scholem had suggested that Jewish mysticism deemphasized normative Rabbinic law. Heschel argued to the contrary, that mysticism was part and parcel of the Rabbinic and Hasidic tradition and that mysticism was deeply rooted in and tied to

Jewish theology and religious practice. The current dominant scholar of Jewish mysticism is Moshe Idel, and Idel, like Heschel before him, challenges Scholem on this issue, arguing that Jewish mysticism and the great historic Jewish mystics were all deeply embedded in and loyal to Jewish religious observance and practice (see Sherwin, 2006). Thus, the polarized split between rational religion and irrational mysticism does not seem to accurately reflect or do justice to the historical development of the Jewish mystical or religious tradition.

Among Freud's greatest achievements was his bringing together enlightenment rationality with romantic subjectivity, the influences of the Greek and the Jewish (Salberg, 2007), Athens and Jerusalem. Freud, however, brought rationality and irrationality together only by splitting them between the method and the object of investigation, between analyst and patient. The psychoanalytic method was meant to be scientific and rational. Fenichel (1941) institutionalized this understanding better than anyone when he declared regarding psychoanalysis, "The subject matter, not the method, of psychoanalysis is irrational" (p. 13). In other words, Freud took from Romanticism the object of his study, irrationality, the unconscious, dreams, femininity, sexuality, the dark depths of the human spirit, but he devised a method and a theory based on Enlightenment rationality that he liked to think of as objective and scientific (see Aron, 2007). Gay (1987) described Freud as "the last of the philosophes" (p. 41).

Just as mainstream Rabbinic or Orthodox Judaism, especially as it had been affected by the *Haskalah*, the Jewish Enlightenment, had tried to create a rational religion, freed of superstitious, irrational, and mystical elements, so too had psychoanalysis attempted to be a rational, scientific psychology. Freud's Enlightenment ideal of science saw it as liberating the individual from the illusion of religion. Psychoanalysis offered Truth as replacement for regressive fantasy. Religious belief was "a lost cause," a "childhood neurosis" (Freud, 1927, p. 53), and Freud paid homage only to "Our god Logos—Reason" (p. 54). But as modern psychoanalytic thinkers and philosophers of science have pointed out, "a more contemporary and nuanced view of science challenges any strict dichotomy between natural science and all other fields, including psychoanalysis and religion" (Jones, quoted in Spezzano & Gargiulo, 1997, p. x). Freud's worship of the god Reason is ironically not supported by the contemporary empirical sciences, which challenge a unitary conception of rationality. Both science and rationality on the one hand and religion and spirituality on the other are more complex and multidimensional than Freud envisioned (Spezzano & Gargiulo, 1997).

Stephen Mitchell's (1993) synthetic integration of relational psychoanalysis offered a strong critique of the dichotomizations of fantasy and reality, illusion and rationality, religion and science. For him, "What is inspiring about psychoanalysis today is not the renunciation of illusion in the hope of joining a common, progressively realistic knowledge and control, but rather the hope of fashioning a personal reality that feels authentic and enriching" (Mitchell, p. 21). With its goal as the enhancement and revitalization of human experience, and in its primary concern with felt meaning, significance, purpose, and value, the sharp division between religion and psychoanalysis diminishes.

But for most of its history, this has not been the attitude of mainstream psychoanalysis. And even in recent years psychoanalytic scholarship, even when deeply sympathetic to religious and mystical experience, has viewed it with suspicion as childish, irrational, and regressive. Among the most sympathetic of psychoanalytic scholars of Jewish mysticism was Mortimer Ostow, whose final book *Spirit, Mind, and Brain: A Psychoanalytic Examination of Spirituality and Religion* affirmatively argued that religion was compatible with psychological health. Ostow tried not to diminish the value of the spiritual journey. One might say that his motto was borrowed from Albert Einstein whom he quoted approvingly: "Science without religion is lame, religion without science is blind" (quoted in Ostow, 2007, p. 4).

Nevertheless, although recognizing its value, Ostow brings an attachment-based psychoanalytic perspective to his understanding of religious and spiritual experience that consistently analyzes its origins in the earliest mother–infant relationship. Experiences that we call spiritual are thought to be "reactivations" of affects from our earliest childhood. I want to remind you of my adolescent experience at the Western Wall where I looked up and heard the voice from the Heavens. And Ostow writes, "The classic prayerful posture is eyes toward the heavens, often with hands held upward as well…. The basis for this behavior can only be the child's upward gaze and upward reach toward the mother, when the child needs to be picked up, rescued.

Help comes from above" (p. 79). I looked up upon hearing, "Also from above will come help."

Ostow writes:

> In the ancient world, religious sites were often set up on hills, for example the Acropolis and the Jerusalem Temple. These places seem to be endowed with an immanent spirituality, often awesome. I believe the reason is that the small child always needs to look up to the mother's face and cries to be lifted in her arms to her shoulder. Above, for the child, is the source of salvation. Demons lurk in the chthonic depth, as the child on the floor is vulnerable to strangers and animals... . What is now the mountain of the Lord was once the mother's shoulder. (p. 100, 107)

Ostow concludes that "Spirituality reflects and retrieves the baby's feeling of attachment to his mother; religion recapitulates and retrieves the older child's feelings and modes of relating to his family" (p. 203). Ostow has moved beyond Freud in several ways. Unlike Freud, he is much more sympathetic to the value of religious experience and much less disdainful. Unlike Freud he traces religious and spiritual experience to the child's earliest attachment to the mother, instead of focusing almost exclusively on the child's oedipal relationship to the father. His analysis of religious and spiritual experience is largely compelling, insightful, and deeply respectful. Nevertheless, in his use of such language as "retrieving," "recapitulating," and "re-activating," Ostow remains in the paradigm of "regression," a return to childish and infantile mental states. There is less emphasis here on "transformation." And it is transformation that becomes the central theme running throughout this cutting-edge book by Karen Starr.

Drawing on a contemporary relational approach to psychoanalysis, and influenced by the work of Stephen Mitchell and others in the relational tradition, Starr views Jewish mystical tradition and spiritual experience in an affirmative spirit, not reduced to something more infantile, childish, primitive, or pathological, but a transformation of these experiences into something new and something significant.

Mitchell (2000), building on and explicating Hans Loewald, suggests that fantasy and reality not be thought of in opposition to each other, but rather as mutually interpenetrating. "There is a sense of enchantment in early experience, and an inevitable disenchantment accompanies the child's growing adaptation to the consensual world of objective reality" (p. 23). For Loewald, and following him, for Mitchell, the objective world of consensual reality is not the only true reality. "Adult reality that has been wholly separated from infantile fantasy is a desiccated meaningless, passionless world" (p. 24).

Contemplating that quiet night in Jerusalem, standing next to the Western Wall, is it best to think of my experience hearing a Heavenly voice as only or predominantly a regressive reactivation of an infantile experience? Or is it also useful to think of it (while not ignoring its childhood origins) as a significant transformation that allowed me for at least one moment to reenchant my world and to infuse it, for ever after, with the meaning and passion of the High Priest, the Holiest official, entering the Holiest space at the Holiest moment of time? Do we view this moment best by reducing it to something earlier or do we understand it better by also recognizing it holistically, as making whole, wholesome, and thus holy?

I hope that you will enjoy Karen Starr's wonderful book, which examines a variety of critical concepts from the perspectives of contemporary psychoanalysis and Jewish mysticism. Allow yourself to be informed and to "learn," to passionately engage these ideas, and to be transformed, and enchanted.

Endnote

1. Elijah was a biblical prophet of the 9th century BCE., who never died but ascended to heaven in a whirlwind. In Jewish and Christian traditions, Elijah is expected to reappear to usher in the Messiah, and in Jewish folklore, Elijah frequently appears in many guises, often helping people in miraculous ways. Eli is short for Elijah, but it also is the short form of my Hebrew name, Eliezer.

References

Aron, L. (2004). God's influence on my psychoanalytic vision and values. *Psychoanalytic Psychology*, 21, 442–451.

Aron, L. (2007). Freud's ironically Jewish science: Commentary on paper by Jill Salberg. *Psychoanalytic Dialogues*, 17(2): 219–231.

Fenichel, O. (1941). *Problems of psychoanalytic technique*. New York: The Psychoanalytic Quarterly.

Freud, S. (1927). The future of an illusion. *Standard Edition*, 21, 1–56. London: Hogarth Press, 1961.

Gay, P. (1987). *A godless Jew*. New Haven, CT: Yale University Press.

Mitchell, S. (2000). *Relationality*. Hillsdale, NJ: The Analytic Press.

Ostow, M. (2007). *Spirit, mind, and brain*. New York: Columbia University Press.

Salberg, J. (2007). Hidden in plain sight: Freud's Jewish identity revisited. *Psychoanalytic Dialogues*, 17(2): 197–217.

Sherwin, B. L. (2006). *Kabbalah*. Lanham, MD: Rowman & Littlefield.

Spezzano, C., & Gargiulo, G. J. (Eds.). (1997). *Soul on the couch*. Hillsdale, NJ: The Analytic Press.

Preface

Although my parents were not orthodox, as a child, I attended an orthodox Jewish day school where I spent half of my school day, every day, studying the Hebrew language, Jewish texts, and the commentaries on those texts. I became absorbed in the Hebrew language, fascinated by the shape of its letters and the roots and meanings of its words. I was intrigued by the rabbinic method of interpretation—the use of association, word play, and *gematria* (numerology with letters) to expand upon the simple, more obvious explanations of the text, and to find deeper meanings. Even then, I was awed by the multiplicity of meanings made possible through interpretation. Later, I experienced this same sense of awe studying literary criticism at Barnard, learning how to deconstruct a text to expose its many possible truths, to find the meaning that resonated with me, and to own and respect that resonance. I bring this experience and love of language to my own work as a writer, a vocation I have pursued since childhood. Most important, I have carried through from childhood the faith in the ability of language to capture experience, and a belief that in the expression of that experience through language, both writer and reader are transformed. This belief carries through to my personal analysis, in which I have experienced firsthand the mutative capacity of language, the transformational power of the right words at the right time.

The question "Where is my place in the world?" is one I have been asking since childhood and that has become more pressing, as I grow older. Despite the traditional rabbinic warning of the possible dangers of studying the Kabbalah before one has reached the maturity that comes with being over 40 (and that one should be married and male), I began exploring the Kabbalah in my twenties. I was drawn to the idea of a meaning beyond me and therefore to me, however, I found the Kabbalah to be elusive and incomprehensible. After finally reaching the ripe old age of 40, I took it up again, and discovered that I was able to begin to grasp some of its concepts without getting a headache.

The writings of the Kabbalah can be frustrating to read from a rational point of view. The texts are often ambiguous, fragmented, and extremely metaphorical. The reader can easily lose her way. However, it is precisely this ambiguity that opens them to interpretation and makes possible a renewed relevance to contemporary discourse. In their vacillation between clarity and obscurity, they mirror the human psychological experience of insight and perplexity. The characters of the Kabbalah make heavy use of elaborate metaphor, a practice that is at once illuminating and obfuscating. The nature of metaphor, indeed its beauty, is that it hints at truths that are not easily accessible through rational language. Metaphor holds the key to unlocking meaning. The unlocking of meaning is also at the heart, and is the art, of the psychoanalytic endeavor.

The problem of transformation has always been a compelling one for me, as I'm sure it is for many of us—whether as patients, therapists, or simply human beings on a soul search. In my own therapy, I remember repeatedly saying, "I *know* this intellectually, but I don't *feel* it inside" and asking what for me was the burning question, "What do I have to *do* in order to change?" Now that I am sitting in the therapist's chair, this is the same question my patients persistently pose to me.

How do people change? Freud wrote of the arduous task of working through, and of the need for the analyst to be patient, and to allow the process to take its course. Bion wrote of the need to remain in mystery and doubt and to be open to experience, to being, rather than knowing. The relational psychoanalytic model posits that it is the relationship between patient and analyst, the mutual striving for understanding in the context of a relationship of mutual, intersubjective recognition that facilitates change. I believe that all these are true, and that they imply a stance of faith, not only on the part of the analyst but also, and equally as important, on the part of the patient.

The Hasidim refer to the necessity when confronted with doubt, of leaping into the abyss and standing in faith. Coincidentally, or perhaps

not so, in response to my question of "How do I change?" r
would tell me rather inscrutably "You have to be willing
abyss." At the time, this answer felt distressingly obscure. But grau
I began to grasp that entering the abyss meant feeling the despair I had
been avoiding, accepting responsibility for my life in its totality, and
perhaps the hardest thing of all, giving up the idea that I had to know
what would happen next. In the kabbalistic formulation this means
attaining, at least for a moment, the *sefira* of *chochma*, or wisdom, in
which one lives in the potentiality of what is and waits for what will
come and what will be. This, for me, is the point of faith.

I have taken Rilke's words to a young poet to heart:

> be patient toward all that is unsolved in your heart and ... try to
> love the questions themselves like locked rooms and like books
> that are written in a very foreign tongue... . And the point is, to
> live everything. Live the questions now. Perhaps you will then
> gradually, without noticing it, live along some distant day into
> the answer. (1934, p. 35)

My interest in both psychoanalytic process and Jewish mystical
thought springs from this love for the questions themselves. This book
is the product of my desire to live the answers into being.

Acknowledgments

Much of the material used in this book was drawn from my doctoral dissertation at Long Island University. I express my heartfelt appreciation to my committee for supporting me in my desire to do a theoretical study that transcends traditional boundaries. In particular, I am grateful to Danielle Knafo, my teacher, advisor, and mentor, whose guidance and support were invaluable, particularly during the times when I found myself struggling to coherently express the inexpressible. Thank you to Robert Keisner, my program director, and to Lewis Aron, who was instrumental in helping me narrow down my topic so that I would not get lost in the vastness of the material.

It is with pleasure that I take this opportunity to especially acknowledge Lewis Aron's contribution in bringing this book to fruition. Lew's participation on my dissertation committee marked the beginning of a mentoring relationship that still stuns me with its graciousness and generosity, characteristics that Lew brings to every encounter. Enthusiastically encouraging me to present my ideas and to pursue publication, Lew has carefully read numerous drafts of my writing, and has been immensely supportive of my scholarship, as well as of my professional development. Embodying the relational values of mutuality with respect for autonomy, he has generously shared his expertise while at the same time making me feel that I am a valued colleague. It is an honor to work with him, and I am delighted that he is now officially my editor.

I thank my agent, Neil Salkind, for channeling his considerable energy and enthusiasm toward bringing my work to the attention of the publishing world. I am particularly grateful to Kate Hawes, Publisher, for valuing the potential of this book. My thanks to Kristopher Spring, assistant editor for his responsiveness, professionalism, and attention to detail, and to the staff of The Analytic Press/Taylor and Francis for all of their help in completing this book. An earlier version of chapter 4 was published in *Psychoanalytic Dialogues,* 2008, 18(2).

My dear friends Elaine Epps, Janet Zinn, Joan Viscardi, and Caryl Frohlich have seen me through numerous transitions over the years; their love and friendship are indispensable to me. Finally, and most important, thank you to my husband, Seth, whose steadfast support of this venture on so many different levels has made it possible for me to live out my dreams; and to my children, Jenna, Rachel, and Benjie, who nourish my soul, and ground me in the sacred details of everyday life.

1. Introduction
The Kabbalah

Madonna's proclamation of herself as a kabbalist, adopting the name Esther to signify her self-described spiritual transformation, has sparked a stampede of celebrities as well as ordinary folk toward the 87 (as of this writing) worldwide Kabbalah Centres established by Philip Berg, formerly known as Feivel Gruberger. An insurance salesman turned spiritual leader, Berg disseminates free copies of the Zohar, the central text of the Kabbalah written in Hebrew and Aramaic, to his adherents, and encourages them to "scan" it, so that they may gain an unconscious understanding of its teachings, as well as a safeguard from evil. The hot Hollywood accessory of the moment is the *bendel*, a bracelet of red string, considered to be imbued with the protection of the Hebrew matriarch Rachel. Used by traditional Jews, the *bendel* was often placed by a mother under the mattress of the crib of her newborn baby to ward off the evil eye. Now available over the Internet for prices ranging from $25.99 to $95, and worn by the likes of Britney Spears and Demi Moore, the "red-string kabbalah bracelet" (Helem, 2004, p. 14) has become a celebrity fashion craze.

The Kabbalah, an ancient term coined over 800 years ago, is gaining widespread familiarity in modern times, thanks in part to Madonna's embrace of this Jewish mystical tradition, vigorously reported in the news media and gossip columns. Passed down orally from teacher to student, the knowledge contained within the Kabbalah was originally kept hidden from all but a select few deemed worthy of receiving it. The word Kabbalah itself means "received" and/or "tradition," reflecting the care that was taken to keep it secret and rooted in *halacha,* Jewish law and religious practice. Equivalent Hebrew words to describe what is known as Jewish mysticism are *sod,* secret, and *chochma nistara,* hidden wisdom. In startling contrast with the esotericism of these traditional teachings and their restriction to a small group of acolytes of exceptional character and meticulous adherence to Jewish practice, the current popularization of the Kabbalah has brought it into the mainstream, making it accessible to the masses without regard to particular religious beliefs or practices. Interest in the Kabbalah by the layperson, rather than the Jewish scholar, has reached astounding proportions. As of this writing, a Google search of "Kabbalah" brings up 4,160,000 results.

A closer examination of the teachings expounded by the Berg family's Kabbalah Centres (Berg, 1988) reveals that they have little to do with the traditional Kabbalah, and much to do with promoting the financial interests of its founders ("The Truth About the Madonna Cult," 2004; Simon, 1998). However, not all of the current fascination with Kabbalah is fashion or fad. There has been a parallel increase in serious study of the original kabbalistic texts. Synagogues offer a growing number of classes in traditional Kabbalah, as does Chabad, the Lubavitch Hasidic movement that has incorporated the Kabbalah's principles into its ethics.

Some of the Kabbalah's ideas have permeated the intellectual mainstream, informing contemporary visions of social justice and environmental responsibility. The goal of *tikkun olam,* repair of the world, has been taken on by Michael Lerner, the founder of *Tikkun Magazine,* as a challenge to effect social change by adding a spiritual dimension to movements such as the women's movement, the gay rights movement, the environmental movement, and the movement for economic justice. The concept of *tikkun* has also infiltrated the field of psychology (Brown, 1997; Kory, 2007), along with the recognition that the psychologist's aim of healing the individual is inexorably linked with the desire to make the world a better place by doing so. The psychologist Laura Brown (1997) characterizes *tikkun olam* as a "core notion informing social justice-oriented practice," exhorting psychologists to "ask themselves, individually and in their organizations, how must they act so as to continue their revolution of healing the world" (p. 461).

Kabbalistic thought is similarly influencing the development of a new trend in contemporary Jewish theology. Arthur Green (1999) argues for a modern reworking of the ancient Jewish doctrine to meet the needs of:

> an environmentally-concerned future that is already upon us. ... The insight that God and universe are related not primarily as Creator and creature, but as deep structure and surface, a central insight of the mystical tradition, is key to the Judaism of the future. But the ways in which we develop and act upon that insight will have to be appropriate to our own age. (Retrieved April 27, 2003. www.tikkun.org/magazine/index.ctm/action/tikkun/issue/tik9909/article/990911.html.)

Albeit at times superficial, the rise of popular interest in the Kabbalah suggests a compelling need in contemporary society for answers to some ancient spiritual questions. In a world rife with fundamentalism, suicide bombings, and terrorism on an international scale, in which "martyrs" surrender their lives to God by killing thousands of innocent people in the process, the call to comprehend the incomprehensible has a renewed relevance. It is no surprise that people seek protection from evil that seems to come out of nowhere. Madonna's "Die Another Day" video, in which she is seen putting on phylacteries containing the name of God while fighting an unidentified enemy, appears to depict the cosmic battle between good and evil, fought on a personal scale. Although it can be considered to be a bastardization of kabbalistic themes, it may on some level tap into the deeper anxieties of an age of fear and uncertainty, in which the threat of apocalyptic annihilation is all too real.

The original flowering of the Kabbalah began during the Middle Ages, a period of similar circumstances of fear and uncertainty for medieval Jewry. Faced with polemics against their minority religion from Christian and Muslim authorities, the Jews were forced to constantly defend their traditions against hostile forces. New intellectual ideas such as Neoplatonism and Aristotelianism also posed a challenge to traditional Judaism, one that was met with a reinterpretation of traditional teachings to incorporate the new ways of thinking. The form that this reinterpretation of the canonized body of Jewish knowledge took was the commentary, a legacy of the Talmudic age (Green, 2004). The Talmud, or body of Jewish law, is itself a commentary on the Torah.

The Kabbalah is essentially creative commentary, a mystical reinterpretation of biblical and rabbinic literature. It can be understood as a radical formulation of a metaphor of creation and the workings of the universe, rooted in traditional Judaism and derived hermeneutically. The kabbalists graphically articulated the view of a mutual relationship between humanity and God as partners in creative process. Because of the divine admonition in the second of the Ten Commandments against "graven images," language was the primary tool with which to articulate this vision. The kabbalists viewed language as the medium through which the world was created, considering the letters of the Hebrew alphabet to be the building blocks of the universe. To them, language was a reflection of the "fundamental, spiritual nature of the world" (Scholem, 1995, p. 17), a window into the soul of the human and the divine. Through their innovative conceptualization of language, the kabbalists raised the interpretive process to new heights of creativity.

This creativity, however, was firmly rooted in the heritage of rabbinic and Talmudic Judaism. Green (2004) distinguishes five elements of Jewish tradition that are evident in the Kabbalah's writings. *Aggadah*, the narrative tradition of the Talmud and the Midrash, is the first of these elements. The *Aggadah* is the teaching of wisdom through the telling of maxims, parables, and fantastic tales, including mythological conceptions of God, and legends of the rabbis. The techniques of interpretation used in the Midrash and appropriated by the kabbalists include finding hidden meanings in the text through the juxtaposition of verses of Scripture, wordplay, and *gematria* or numerology, the assignment of numerical values to individual letters. Through this process of interpretation, the kabbalists believed that they could derive unifying, cosmic structures from the words of the Torah. In fact, the Torah itself was believed by the kabbalists to be the divine in word, a linguistic manifestation of God. It was conceived as a living organism, containing within it an infinity of meanings, all of which are interpretations of what is hidden (Scholem, 1991).

The second element is *halacha,* Jewish law. The early kabbalists were schooled in *halacha* and lived strictly within its boundaries. Much of their teaching sprang from their desire to transform Jewish religious practice from intellectualized, rote performance to vibrant ritual, alive with spiritual meaning and capable of cosmic effect. Practice of Jewish law was seen as a tool for enabling *tikkun,* repair of the world, a task that could be accomplished only by humanity on the physical plane. It is the Kabbalah's "relation to the spiritual heritage of rabbinical Judaism," says Scholem, that is the secret to its success. "This relation differs from that of rationalist philosophy, in that it is more deeply and in a more vital sense connected with the main forces active in Judaism" (1995, p. 23).

The liturgy comprises the third element. The kabbalists deemed these texts of poetry and prayer worthy of interpretation and commentary, and paid great attention to the spiritual intention, or *kavanah,* behind each prayer. Indeed, the Friday night service welcoming the "Sabbath bride," recited to this day in modern Jewish congregations, was composed by the kabbalists of Safed in the 16th century, and is replete with kabbalistic themes. These prayers vividly depict the relationship between humanity and God as that of beloved soul mates and reflect the kabbalistic yearning for union of the masculine and feminine aspects of the divine. *Merkavah,* or chariot, mysticism, which predated the Kabbalah, is the fourth element. Originating from the prophetic "chariot" visions of Ezekiel, *Merkavah* mysticism is characterized by mystical praxis with the goal of attaining a vision of God. The fifth element is the *Sefer Yetzirah,* a proto-kabbalistic work that develops an abstract conceptualization of cosmic unity through the contemplation of the meaning of numbers and letters. It is in *Sefer Yetzirah* that the doctrines of the *sefirot,* the attributes of God, and the *otiyot yesod,* the foundational letters held to be the "pillars of the universe," first appear.

The Kabbalah proper is said to originate in 12th-century Provence, with the appearance of the *Sefer HaBahir,* an anonymously authored book of language mysticism (Scholem, 1987). The Kabbalah rapidly spread to Spain, where the Zohar, the central text of the Kabbalah, was "discovered" by Moses de Leon in 1286. Although de Leon attributed the Zohar to Shimon Bar Yohai, a rabbi of the 2nd century, modern scholars believe that de Leon himself was the Zohar's author. The Zohar, for the most part a commentary on the five books of Moses, contains discourses on the process of creation, the nature of good and evil, the composition of the human soul, and the attributes of God.

A stunning revival of kabbalistic thought took place in the 16th century in the town of Safed (known as Tzfat in modern-day Israel). Moses Cordovero (1522–1570) and Isaac Luria (1534–1572) developed strikingly original theosophical systems, founded on the ideas articulated in the Zohar. Cordovero developed a system of ordering the *sefirot,* values or archetypes, and posited that the *sefirot* were not only attributes of God, but were also aspects of the human soul, which was, in the words of the Bible, "fashioned in God's image (*tzelem Elohim*)" (Genesis 1:27). The implication of this concept is that the journey to search for God must be traveled on the path to self-understanding.

Luria's oral teachings, written down by his student, Chaim Vital (1543–1620), form the complex and innovative theosophical system of thought known as the Lurianic Kabbalah. Luria's ideas stand in contrast with those of prior kabbalists, who had developed a theory of creation based on language and emanation. The creation metaphor articulated by Isaac Luria is roughly as follows: God is a paradoxical union of being and no-thing, of *Ein-sof,* without end, and *ayin,* nothingness. *Ein-sof* made creation possible through a negative act of contraction or withdrawal, *tzimtzum,* leaving a void. Into this void emanated the *sefirot,* archetypes of values and ways of being. These *sefirot* are contained in vessels, said by earlier kabbalists to be composed of the 22 letters (the Hebrew alphabet) of divine speech.

Unable to contain the divine light they were meant to contain, the vessels shattered, creating broken shards that tumbled through the void, entrapping sparks of light in husks, *klippot,* that form the lower worlds, including the world of evil, referred to by Luria as *sitra achra,* the other side. Evil, separated from its source, but still encapsulating light, takes on a life and energy of its own, perpetuating itself, and wreaking havoc upon humanity. In the higher worlds, the masculine and feminine aspects of the divine were driven apart, disrupting the flow of erotic energy in all the worlds. Some of the divine light, not trapped in *klippot,* returned to its source, beginning a process of repair, or *tikkun.* Humanity's role in this cosmic drama is to continue the process of *tikkun.*

Luria's ideas are unique in viewing humanity in partnership with God in the creative process, and as participating in a continuous dialogue with the divine. By contracting, God in effect made room for the world, humanity, and human free will. *Tikkun olam,* repair of the world, is completed by humankind, whose task it is to elevate the sparks, reuniting the masculine and feminine aspects of God. The Kabbalah holds that the universe is comprised of many worlds of varying dimensions. Humanity's domain is the physical world, and so it is humankind's moral, intellectual, and spiritual acts, including acts of social justice, that effect *tikkun* in all the worlds (Steinsaltz, 1980). In this manner, the human being acts as God's partner in creation of the world, and is said even to transform God Himself.

2. Psychoanalysis and the Kabbalah
A Case for Dialogue

In working with people to bring them to themselves, one must work at great depth, a depth scarcely imaginable.

Rabbi Nachman of Bratzlav

Psychoanalysis, "the talking cure," and the Kabbalah, a work of exegesis, are both predicated on the belief in the human capacity for transformation. Each has faith in the creative and reparative powers of language, particularly within the context of relationship. In psychoanalytic discourse, the problem of transformation has been the subject of much debate since Freud defined the goal of analysis to be the making of the unconscious conscious, declaring, "Where id was there shall ego be." As psychoanalytic thinking has evolved from a one-person psychology to a two-person psychology, there has been an increasing emphasis on the role of the analytic relationship in facilitating psychic change. Whereas the traditional model of classical psychoanalysis has been to bring to awareness the memories and events buried in the unconscious that will reveal the childhood roots of conflict, the contemporary focus is much more on creating an environment of interpersonal intimacy from which a deeply personal sense of authenticity may emerge (Epstein, 1996). Rather than viewing the analyst as objective observer, blank slate, or reflecting mirror, contemporary psychoanalysis acknowledges that the analytic process affects both participants in the dyad, the analyst as well as the patient.

The Kabbalah's metaphors of transformation offer a vivid and potentially illuminating framework with which to reconsider the transformational experience within psychoanalytic process, as well as the evolving view within psychoanalysis of the relationship between analyst and analysand as one of asymmetry and mutuality (Aron, 1996). In their formulation of transformation in terms of the individual's mutual relationship with God, the kabbalists succeeded in articulating a dimension of experience that I believe has eluded psychoanalysis's grasp. In drawing on these kabbalistic metaphors, my intent is to more clearly discern and articulate this spiritual perspective of mutuality with the aim of contributing to the psychoanalytic understanding of psychic change in a relational context.

Psychologists and scholars of Jewish textual criticism have noted striking parallels between several kabbalistic and psychoanalytic concepts, but have only recently begun to study them. While Ostow (1995) urges "psychoanalytic study of the Kabbalah as a serious discipline" (p. xiii), the published work in the field is sparse, at best. The Kabbalah's sexual metaphors have been examined from a Freudian perspective (Ostow, 1995), and its notion of *tikkun* contrasted with the Kleinian concept of reparation (Lutzky, 1989). Arguing for a contemporary interpretation of the ancient kabbalistic symbols, Drob (2000a, b) undertakes a sweeping comparative study of kabbalistic themes with several philosophical and psychological concepts, but his broad focus precludes a detailed examination of how these ideas might be applied to the specifics of the psychoanalytic situation. Of central importance to an exploration of the interface between ancient tradition and present-day discourse, modern Kabbalah scholarship (Idel, 2002) and the recent translations of kabbalistic texts from their original Hebrew/Aramaic (Matt, 2004a, b) have brought them out of the obscurity of esotericism and made them accessible to investigation through the medium of contemporary thought.

My goal is to continue the task of enrichment through mutual dialogue by examining in depth the relevance of the Kabbalah's metaphors of transformation to the psychoanalytic endeavor. I believe that an exploration of these themes will provide a richer and more expansive perspective from which to view the transformational, and at times even spiritual, aspects of the psychoanalytic situation. It has been noted that whereas religion creates a myth of the external world, psychoanalysis creates a myth of the internal world, an organizing model that creates "order out of the chaotic givenness of human existence" (Spezzano & Gargiulo, 1997, p. xiv). In opening a conversation between the Kabbalah and contemporary psychoanalytic theory, I hope to demonstrate that "discourses about the soul and the discourses of the couch could inform, and not simply argue with or ignore one another" (p. xiv).

A work of creative exegesis, the Kabbalah is well suited for a dialogue with contemporary psychoanalysis. Levenson notes that the Jewish hermeneutical tradition, like the interpersonal paradigm, undertakes "the making explicit of what is hidden" (Levenson, 1995, p. 1), concerning itself with the "detailed inquiry" (Sullivan, 1953) and "the pursuit of the particular" (Levenson, 1988).[1] Relevant to the evolving view within psychoanalysis of a two-person psychology, with its roots in interpersonal theory (Aron, 1990), the Kabbalah emphasizes the role of relationship in facilitating transformation. As Aron (2004) has demonstrated, "The relational emphases on mutuality and asymmetry have structural parallels in Jewish theological formulations" (p. 449). Significantly, in the Kabbalah, which is rooted in traditional Judaism, the desire for relationship is intrinsic to transformation. Indeed, the motivation for Creation itself is attributed to God's longing to be known and recognized by the human being! Somewhat radically for a theosophical system, the moment of transformation is perceived as a mutual encounter in which both parties, the human being *and God,* are transformed.

Relevant to psychoanalytic discourse, the Kabbalah identifies a yearning for personal transformation, equating it with the arousal of desire for self-understanding and self-expansion. It speaks of the divine spark that is clothed within a person's soul, hidden from conscious awareness, yet longing to be perceived and enflamed. The Kabbalah characterizes the journey toward self-understanding and self-realization as *tikkun,* or repair, by which the particular spark unique to one's soul is enflamed and restored to its source in the divine, transforming God Himself in the process. The endeavor to know the self deeply is conceived as the movement toward God in relationship. Reciprocally, through being sought out and recognized by the human being, God Himself is brought into balance.

The Dual Nature of Human Inquiry

The writings of the Kabbalah embody the dual nature of human inquiry—outward into the cosmos, and inward into the soul. Like psychoanalysis, the Kabbalah is a search for meaning, a reflection of the human being's struggle for balance between inner and outer life. The kabbalists sought to know God through knowing themselves. Likewise, there are analysts who write of experiencing in psychoanalysis something of the sacred (Eigen, 1981, 1985, 1998; Garguilo & Spezzano, 1997; Sorenson, 2004) and of their religious and psychoanalytic views mutually informing one another (Aron, 2004).

Despite his characterization of himself as a rational atheist, Freud chose the word *psyche,* which translates best as soul, rather than mind or brain, to describe the subject of psychoanalytic inquiry (Bettelheim, 1984). Jung held that psychotherapy of necessity must address the philosophical yearnings of the soul, contending "one cannot treat the psyche without touching on man and life as a whole, including the ultimate and deepest issues" (Jung, 1929, p. 76). The dual nature of humanity's desire to "know" about the universe and about itself is most familiarly evident in the story of Adam and Eve. After eating from the Tree of Knowledge, Adam and Eve attempt to hide from God, who asks, "Where are you?" The Kabbalah, like the psychoanalytic endeavor, is an attempt to answer this question—where is one's place in the world (Steinsaltz, 1980)?

The drawing of parallels between the writings of the Kabbalah and the psychology of the human mind predate the psychoanalytic inquiry. In their development of the *sefirot,* the symbols through which the kabbalists attempted to apprehend the attributes of God, they acknowledged that these symbols were an incomplete representation, grounded in human perception and conceptualization. Believing that the microcosm mirrors the macrocosm, they interpreted the biblical statement that God made man in his image to mean that the creative and transformational processes of the cosmos are reflected in, and are affected by, those of the human psyche. From the perspective of modern psychology, the *sefirot* may be viewed as the kabbalists' attempt to express psychological concepts that did not yet exist. Yet by embedding the search for the self in the larger context of the individual's contribution to the universal, the kabbalists gave expression to a spiritual and moral basis for an endeavor that in modern times (in the form of psychoanalysis), has been criticized for its focus on the individual to the exclusion of one's relation to the larger whole.

The Hasidic masters of the 18th and 19th centuries popularized the Kabbalah's ideas by interpreting its symbols and metaphors in philosophical and psychological terms and applying them to psychological processes within the individual. They developed moral and ethical guidelines for living that are practiced to this day, particularly within the Chabad, or Lubavitch branch. (The name Chabad is an acronym for *chochma, binah,* and *daat,* the sefirotic attributes of wisdom, understanding, and knowledge). In the Hasidic tradition, the *rebbe* serves as both a spiritual and psychological counselor. The task of the *rebbe* in counseling is to help the individual seeker to live up to his unique purpose—in kabbalistic terms, the root of his soul. Living true to the unique nature of one's soul is considered to be the unique contribution of the individual to the universal, and indeed, the very purpose of one's existence. Before his death, Hasidic master Rabbi Zusya of Hanipol is said to have declared, "In the coming world, they will not ask me: 'Why were you not Moses?' They will ask me: 'Why were you not Zusya?'" (Buber, 1947, p. 251).

The *Tanya,* written by Rabbi Schneur Zalman of Liadi in the late 18th century, is one of the fundamental works of Hasidism. It addresses in detail the moral and ethical implications of kabbalistic teachings, with a particular emphasis on the struggle between good and evil in the human soul. The central innovation of the *Tanya* is its conception of the *beinoni,* or "in between" person. The *beinoni* is neither righteous nor evil, nor even somewhere in between. Instead, the state of the *beinoni* is conceptualized as a condition of ongoing tension within the individual, who is pulled between the two opposing natures of his or her soul: the part that draws downward toward the earth, and the aspect that aspires upward toward the divine:

> The conflict, then, is not a war of annihilation, in which man seeks to destroy certain parts of his soul; rather it is an effort to educate all the parts of the human soul, to create within them a

consciousness and a feeling—until their aspirations merge with those of the divine soul, so that the person reaches a state of perfect harmony between body and soul, the earthly and the divine. (Steinsaltz, 2003, p. xiv)

A corollary of the *Tanya*'s teaching is that the successful balancing of this state of tension is attainable by the average person. It is precisely for the purpose of this struggle, holds the *Tanya*, that humankind was created. According to Schneur Zalman, a complete psychological analysis of a person would include not only an exploration of his animal soul, in other words, his animal drives and instincts, but also of his divine soul, which clothes his "divine spark," this particular individual's unique contribution to the world. The kabbalists referred to this divine soul as the *tzelem* (Scholem, 1991), which is both the unique, purposive, essence of a person on the worldly plane (embodying the specific meaning of his existence) and its spiritual counterpart on the celestial plane. This spiritual counterpart emerges from the source of the individual's being and serves as a guide to him, particularly in the meditative state, to raising the spark contained within the core of his being (Drob, 2000a). In more modern terminology, the *tzelem* might be equated with the person's sense of authenticity, of being true to the meaning of her existence. This concept and its relevance to contemporary psychoanalytic thinking will be explored further later on.

Perhaps the most eloquent modern interpreter of kabbalistic principles as applied to the human situation is the Jewish philosopher Martin Buber. Although Buber was raised in the context of the Enlightenment values of intellectual reasoning and rationality, as a child, his father often took him to visit the Hasidic community of Sadagora in Galicia (Friedman, 2002). When, at the age of 26, Buber found himself in spiritual and creative crisis, he steeped himself in Hasidic texts for 5 years, emerging from his isolation with renewed vigor. In addition to his philosophy of dialogue, Buber is best known for bringing Hasidic thought and culture to the awareness of the Western world. His *Tales of the Hasidim* (Buber, 1947) is the definitive collection of the Hasidic legends and stories through which Hasidic thinking is made manifest, and that greatly influenced Buber's later philosophical thought. Buber was interested in Eastern and German mysticism as well as Jewish mysticism, and retained many of these mystical elements in his existential philosophy and his later philosophy of dialogue. His emphasis on the importance of discernment and continual attunement to one's "unique purpose" and his views on the redemption of evil are clearly rooted in kabbalistic and Hasidic thinking.

Buber (1999) had much to say about psychoanalysis and psychotherapy (Buber, 1999), criticizing both behaviorism and Freud's mechanistic orientation for giving themselves over to pure subject-object knowledge of man. He objected as well to Jung's veneration of the individuation of the self as the ultimate goal of analytic psychotherapy, maintaining that psychotherapy and psychoanalysis must be grounded in a realistic conception of what it means to human—including not only the individual's unique personality and neuroses, but also giving equal weight to the individual's relation to others. He held that

> One who understands the essence of man in terms of the dialogical relation between men must walk a narrow ridge between the individualistic psychology which places all reality within the isolated individual and the social psychology which places all reality in the organic group and in the interaction of social forces. (Friedman, 2002, p. 217)

The "narrow ridge" is the crux of Buber's dialogic philosophy, his metaphor for "genuine personal meetings in the abyss of human existence" (p. 19). Notably, Erich Fromm, likely influenced directly by Buber through his membership in the Frankfurt circle of students of the Bible and Judaism led by Buber and Franz Rosenzweig (Friedman, 2002), redefined psychology's focus to be "that of the specific kind of relatedness of the individual towards the world and not that of the satisfaction or frustration of this or that instinctual need per se" (Fromm, 1994, p. 10). Ehrenberg (1974) draws heavily upon Buber's ideas in her conceptualization of the "intimate edge" of the psychoanalytic encounter, as does Aron (1996) in his explication of mutuality in a relational context.

Historical Context of Kabbalah Scholarship

Gershom Scholem's extensive and groundbreaking scholarship (Scholem, 1969, 1987, 1991, 1995) brought the Kabbalah out of the obscurity of medieval Jewish esotericism and into the wider circle of modern intellectual ideas. A historian, Scholem analyzed the kabbalistic texts from the perspective of Jewish history, viewing the Kabbalah as a closed system, one whose symbols were impenetrable to interpretation via rational thought. Scholem believed that the mystical symbol "in itself, through its own existence ... makes another reality transparent which cannot appear in any other form" and "is an expressible representation of something which lies beyond the sphere of expression and communication" (1995, p. 27).

Scholem did not attempt comparative studies of the Kabbalah, concentrating only on the admittedly formidable task of elucidating its texts, ideas, and historical development within the context of Jewish thought. Although Scholem was familiar with the theories of Freud and Jung, he specifically chose not to explicate the Kabbalah using psychoanalytic concepts or terminology (Biale, 1982), preferring instead to leave that undertaking to psychologists. Following Scholem, modern critical scholarship in Judaic studies has traditionally been wary of "alien proposals" such as psychoanalysis for understanding Jewish texts, and "simply does not allow certain questions on its agenda" (Halperin, 1995, p. 183). Scholem himself, however, concluded *On the Kabbalah and its Symbolism* with the words, " ... the historian's task ends where the psychologist's begins" (1969, p. 204). Psychology may read this as an exhortation to take up these questions for *its* agenda, and it is in the spirit of Scholem's words that this book sets out to do so.

Influence of Jewish Mystical Thought on Psychoanalytic Theory

The similarity between a number of kabbalistic and psychoanalytic concepts has spawned considerable speculation regarding the influence of Jewish mystical thought on Freud's ideas, accounted for by his close relationship with his father, Jacob, who was raised as a Hasid (Bakan, 1958; Drob 2000a, 2000b; Merkur, 1997; Roback, 1957). Freud was concerned about "the danger of [psychoanalysis] becoming a Jewish national affair" (Freud & Abraham, 1965, p. 34) and did not publicly acknowledge indebtedness to Jewish ideas. In fact, he vehemently resisted the implication that his work had anything whatsoever to do with religion, attributing all of his discoveries to the scientific method (Meng & Freud, 1963).

There has been much debate regarding Freud's identification as a Jew and his desire to distance himself from the bindings of traditional religion (Salberg, 2007). However, biographical research into Freud's upbringing indicates not only that he was schooled in Jewish culture, but also that he was of Hasidic descent, and more than likely familiar with the concepts inherent in Hasidic tradition (Philp, 1956; Roback, 1957). Roazen (1975) likens Freud's attitude toward his patients to that of a rabbi toward his followers, and reports that Freud was known to recount Hasidic tales in the course of clinical practice.[2]

David Bakan, in *Sigmund Freud and the Jewish Mystical Tradition* (1958) was the first to attempt to make a connection between Freud's family background and his use of kabbalistic ideas in formulating his theories. Unfortunately, Bakan's thesis that Freud identified with the militant messianism of Shabbatai Tzvi, the kabbalistically inspired false messiah, is fantastic and speculative and ultimately unbelievable. However, Bakan successfully demonstrates that Freud identified as a Jew in an increasingly anti-Semitic milieu, and convincingly contends that this atmosphere of hostility toward Jews contributed to Freud's denial of any Jewish origin to psychoanalysis. He also makes a strong argument for considering Freud's use of interpretation in the analysis of individuals to be an application of the Jewish technique of interpretation of the Torah.

Bakan reports little direct evidence of Freud's scholarly interest in the Kabbalah, with one exception: an interesting anecdote in the preface to a second edition of his book. After the publication of his first edition, Bakan was approached by Rabbi Chaim Bloch, who described an encounter he had had with Freud. Rabbi Bloch reported that, recognizing the psychological significance of a manuscript of Chaim Vital, a kabbalist of the 16th and 17th centuries who compiled Isaac Luria's teachings in written form, he approached Freud to ask him to write a foreword to it and assist him in its publication.

"Freud, said Chaim Bloch, was beside himself with excitement on reading the manuscript. 'This is gold,' Freud said, and asked why Chaim Vital's work had never been brought to his attention before" (Bakan, 1958, p. xix). Freud, in turn, showed the manuscript of *Moses and Monotheism* to Rabbi Bloch, who responded, "Anti-Semites accuse us of killing the founder of Christianity. Now a Jew adds that we also killed the founder of Judaism. You are digging a trap for the Jewish people" (Bakan, 1965, p. xix). This response reportedly so incensed

Freud that he walked out of the room, leaving Rabbi Bloch alone in his library. Not wanting to be impolite and leave immediately, Rabbi Bloch perused the books on Freud's shelves, and noted that among his Judaica collection were several German language books on Jewish mysticism, as well as a French translation of the Zohar, the central text of the Kabbalah.[3]

Daniel Merkur (1997) definitively draws a Hasidic connection between Freud's ideas and the Kabbalah:

> Surely it was no coincidence that in the authentic teaching of the Baal Shem Tov [the founder of the Hasidic movement] we find the basic assumptions of Freud's technique of psychotherapy: that it is permissible to think wicked thoughts, that wicked fantasies cannot be helped, that the main thing to do is not to avoid the fantasies, but to defuse them by interpreting them and gaining insight into their proper meaning. Have we reason to doubt that Jacob Freud communicated the tolerant attitudes of Hasidic ethics in advising his son how to manage his family life? (p. 20)

Merkur contrasts the kabbalistic and psychoanalytic concepts of sexuality, and contends that Freud provided a psychological interpretation for the notion that had long been espoused by the Kabbalah and accepted by the Hasidim, of latent sexuality as a driving universal force. He draws attention, as well, to the similarities between Hasidism's and psychoanalysis's view of parapraxes as symbolic events that should be interpreted, and maintains that Freud adopted this Hasidic concept and incorporated it into his theories.

A review of the biographical data (Bakan, 1958; Meng and Freud, 1963; Merkur, 1997; Philp, 1956; Roback, 1957) regarding the possibility of Freud's familiarity with Kabbalah leads one to conclude that it is unlikely that Freud consciously incorporated Jewish mystical ideas into his theories. However, it is almost certain that he was exposed to these ideas and influenced by them.

There is strong evidence that Jung perceived a kinship between Jewish mysticism and psychoanalytic ideas (Drob, 2000a). Jung (1963) suggested that a complete understanding of the significance of Freud's Jewish descent with regard to his theories "would carry us beyond

Jewish orthodoxy into the subterranean workings of Hasidism and then into the intricacies of the Kabbalah, which still remains unexplored psychologically" (p. 359). He acknowledged his acquaintance with the Christian Kabbalah, particularly the writings of Knorr Von Rosenroth, who translated passages of the Zohar and other kabbalistic works into Latin. Jung also found inspiration in Moses Cordovero's *Pardes Rimonim*, a kabbalistic text he cites in *Mysterium Coniunctionis* (1963), his last major work. In a letter to the Reverend Erastus Evans, he writes:

> In a tract of the Lurianic Kabbalah, the remarkable idea is developed that man is destined to become God's helper in the attempt to restore the vessels which were broken when God thought to create a world. Only a few weeks ago, I came across this impressive doctrine, which gives meaning to man's status exalted by the incarnation. I am glad that I can quote at least one voice in favor of my rather involuntary manifesto. (Jung, 1975, cited in Drob, 2000a, p. 289)

Wilfred Bion used the sign 'O' to denote, variously, the emotional reality of the moment, ultimate reality, absolute truth, the ineffable "no-thing," the infinite and formless void—all attributes of what the kabbalists called *Ein-sof* (the name for God meaning infinite or without end) or *ayin* (no-thing). In stark contrast to Freud's scientific positivism, Bion created a numinous psychoanalytic epistemology that challenged the prevailing psychoanalytic tradition. In its prescription for approaching the psychoanalytic situation in a state of free-floating attention, "without memory or desire," Bion's epistemology was more mystical than traditionally scientific in nature. Acutely aware of his own revolutionary impact on the psychoanalytic establishment, Bion likened it to the impact of the Kabbalah (specifically Isaac Luria and his ideas) on the rabbinical directorate. In his discussion of the mystic and the group (Bion, 1977c), he explicitly draws an analogy between himself and Luria, and between his ideas and those of the Kabbalah. Like Buber, Bion was also interested in Eastern mysticism and the writings of the German mystic Meister Eckhart. The relevance of Bion's contributions to this study will be further elaborated in the next chapter.

Endnotes

1. For a thorough discussion of the relevance of the Jewish interpretive tradition to contemporary psychoanalysis, see Aron, 2007.

2. Hanns Sachs, a Viennese Jewish analyst and a colleague of Freud's, on moving to America and treating more non-Jewish than Jewish patients, was worried about how he could continue analyzing without these stories. His solution was to substitute a minister for the rabbi in these tales. "I baptize the stories," he said (Roazen, 1975, p. 15).

3. Interestingly, Rabbi Bloch admitted to Bakan that his "evil impulse" had caused him to toy with the idea of switching manuscripts, so that *Moses and Monotheism* would be gone forever. He only resisted because of the thought that Freud might have another copy!

3. Transformation

They asked the Rabbi of Lublin: "Why in the Zohar is the turning to God which corresponds to the *sefira* 'understanding' called 'Mother?'" The Rabbi of Lublin explained, "When a man's heart accepts understanding and turns toward it, he becomes like a new-born child, and his own turning to God is his mother." (Buber, 1947, p. 314)

transform: 1. To change the form of, specifically: a. To change in outward shape or semblance; b. To change in structure or composition; c. To change in nature, disposition, heart, or the like. 2. *Elec.* To change in potential or in type. 3. *Math.* To change the form of, as an algebraic expression or geometrical figure, without altering the meaning or value. 4. *Physics.* To change one form of energy into another.

The Aims of Analysis

The process of transformation has been the central preoccupation of psychoanalysis since its inception, when Freud (1894) first posited that anxiety arose as "a transformation out of ... accumulated sexual tension" (p. 191) and then continued to pursue his study of the variety of transformations—of libido, of memory, of affect, to name only a few—involved in the ways individuals cope with reality and with the instinctual demands of their internal worlds. Freud (1940) drew his analogies from the natural sciences, proposing that, "in mental life some kind of energy is at work" (p. 163) and maintaining that psychic processes comprise dynamic transformations in energy from one form to another. Freud defined the goal of analysis as being to "transform what has become unconscious and repressed into preconscious material and thus return it once more to the possession of [the patient's] ego" (p. 181). Through this process, the ego is strengthened, as the energy that it had previously consumed in its attempts to fend off the demands of the id, is returned to it for fulfilling the task of coping with reality.

Language is the primary vehicle for transforming unconscious material into consciousness. It was Freud's investigation of trauma that gave birth to psychoanalysis, with Freud concluding that language is the mutative agent in the amelioration of traumatic symptoms (Breuer & Freud, 1893). He found that it is *the telling,* with affect, that rids the body of the symptom. When memories return in the form of images, they must be transformed through language:

> Once a picture has emerged from the patient's memory, we may hear him say that it becomes fragmentary and obscure in proportion as he proceeds with his description of it. *The patient is, as it were, getting rid of it by turning it into words.* (p. 280)

The recall of memory, Freud discovered, requires a state of mind quite different from conscious reflection—a state of nonjudgmental receptivity uncontrolled by will, a passive or meditative rather than active state. Freud's method of free association called upon the patient to dissociate from conscious thinking, "from everything, in short, on which he can employ his will" (p. 271) and to instead allow the psychic processes to appear before him, observe them, and put them into words.

Implicit in psychoanalytic formulations of transformation or psychic change are assumptions regarding the goals of analysis. How one conceives of psychic change depends in part on how one answers the question, "What does analysis seek to cure?" However, it is questionable whether "cure" is the appropriate term with which to capture the essence of a successful analysis. Freud (1937) himself acknowledged the difficulty of judging when, if ever, an analysis could be considered complete. Although he described the aims of analysis as the making conscious of repressed material, thereby relieving symptoms and preventing a "repetition of the pathological processes concerned" (p. 219), he questioned whether it was possible to attain the more ambitious goal of guaranteeing a level of "psychic normality" that would remain stable over time, after analysis had been ended. With the aid of analysis, the ego can be strengthened and its control over the instincts improved, but, according to Freud, this transformation is quantitative, a matter of degree, and might never be fully accomplished. "The transformation is achieved, but often only partially: portions of the old mechanisms remain untouched by the work of analysis" (p. 229). Freud pragmatically concludes, "The business of the analysis is to secure the best possible psychological conditions for the functions of the ego; with that it has discharged its task" (p. 250).

Freud (1914) warned that psychic change can be an "arduous task" for the patient and a "trial of patience" for the analyst (p. 155), and cautioned that simply naming the resistance and making it known to the patient, although necessary, is not sufficient to mobilize change. Working through, Freud maintained, effects the greatest changes in the patient and is the primary feature that distinguishes psychoanalysis from suggestion. The patient must grapple with the resistance by continuing the analytic work in defiance of it, whereas "the doctor has nothing else to do than to wait and let things take their course, a course which cannot be avoided nor always hastened" (p. 155). Psychic change, in other words, requires struggle and perseverance against the resistance, on the one hand, and patience, receptivity, and faith in the analytic process, on the other, lest the analysis be aborted prematurely.

Transformation in Religious Experience

Long before its use in psychoanalysis, the term "transformation" has been associated with religious experience, with a connotation more qualitative than quantitative. Individuals are said to be transformed by encounters with the divine, emerging with a sense of a reality greater than themselves, a more expansive perspective of life's possibilities, and a sharper perception of their own unique purpose. In the Torah, such a transformation is often marked by a change in name: at the moment of entering into relationship with God through His covenant, Abram becomes Abraham and his wife Sarai becomes Sarah, signifying that the elderly, childless couple (Abraham is 99, Sarah, 90) will be patriarchs of a great nation.

The night before he is to meet with his estranged and presumably hostile brother Esau, Jacob wrestles with a mysterious figure until dawn. From the story, it is never clear whether it is a man, angel, God, or an aspect of Jacob himself; the text is ambiguous and so is open to interpretation. Jacob's conflict does not leave him unscathed, but it does leave him richer for the experience. Jacob emerges from his encounter with a wound in his thigh and a lifelong limp, but also with an expanded perception of himself and his relationship with his brother. He is given the name Israel—"wrestles with God"—to mark the struggle as well as the suffering that is the turning point of his transformation.

Jacob's new name also signifies the manner in which he has changed. When we first meet Jacob, he is characterized as a simple man, a tent-dweller, a man who, at the moment of his birth, grabbed on to the heel of his twin brother Esau, and then in later years proceeded to steal his brother's birthright through deceiving his elderly, blind father. His name, Yaakov in Hebrew, has as its root the word "heel;" the Zohar interprets its meaning as "deceiver" (Matt, 2004b, p. 270). Because of his treachery, Jacob lived in fear of being killed by Esau, who was much stronger and more aggressive than he. But on this day, Jacob set out toward Esau, prepared to meet his brother face to face, not knowing what the outcome would be—whether he would live or die. The name Israel signifies an added dimension to Jacob's identity, encompassing a newfound willingness to come to terms with his prior actions, to grapple with their consequences, and to tolerate the unknown of a new way of relating. He is different, somehow larger, than he was before. Interestingly, it is the agent of Jacob's transformation, the mysterious figure who struggles with him, who gives Jacob the name Israel. By naming him, he helps Jacob to grasp the emotional essence of what he has just gone through and to understand that he has been changed by it.

In turn, Jacob puts words to his ineffable experience by giving the scene of his transformation a name. He calls the place Peniel—"I have seen God face to face." By naming it, he acknowledges the revelatory nature of his experience and seeks its affirmation through linking his changed inner reality to the concrete outer reality of place. In psychoanalytic terms, naming is Jacob's way of processing an experience that was most certainly traumatic—painful, but also numinous; putting his experience into words helps him not only to understand it but also to assign it a transformative meaning, enabling him to go forth a changed person. Through his struggle, Jacob has come face to face with God and, in the process, face to face with a heretofore-unexpressed aspect of himself. Or perhaps it is the reverse—through Jacob's knowing himself more deeply, God is revealed.

Change of name or place also may signify transformation through acts of passionate will (Zornberg, 1995). Maimonides, in describing transformation through repentance, or *teshuva* (its literal translations are *return, turning toward,* and *response*), writes, "The penitent should ... change his name, as if to say, I am another, I am not the same person who did those things" (Rambam, Mishneh Torah, Hilkhot Teshuva 2:4). The Talmud (B. Rosh Hashanah 16b) discusses transformation in connection with Rosh Hashanah, the Jewish New Year, the day that marks the anniversary of the creation of the world and that begins a 10-day period of introspection and self-examination culminating in Yom Kippur, the Day of Atonement. Here, transformation is intimately connected with creation, with the human desire to recreate the self anew and to thereby participate in the cosmic creative process. The 10-day period of *teshuva* creates a space in time for transitioning from the old year to the new, for the shedding of old patterns of behavior for new possibilities of relating.

Steinsaltz (1980) notes that some kabbalists held that *teshuva* was created even before the world itself, and is a primordial, universal phenomenon that is embedded in its structure. The implication of this idea is that human beings were created with the potential to change the direction of their lives. Even in the dimension of time, which flows inexorably, and in which the past is fixed, people have a measure of control over their own existence, the possibility of changing the significance of the past in the context of the present and future. *Teshuva* is thus the highest expression of the human capacity to choose freely, embodying the ability to transcend the chain of causality. It is no less than a manifestation of the divine in the human.

A Kabbalistic Example of Transformation

"*Lech lecha,*" God commands Abraham in Genesis, simply translated as "Go forth." In its plain meaning, Abraham's journey is the classic prototype of transformation through change of place. However, the Zohar interprets *"Lech lecha"* hyperliterally, as an imperative for personal transformation: "Go to yourself, to know yourself, to refine yourself" (Matt, 2004a, p. 9). The Zohar reads God's directive as a call for Abraham not only to physically move away from the land of his birth, but to leave all that is familiar and to which he has clung and to begin a process of self-examination that will take him out of his current existential situation into a new paradigm of being. But although the paradigm is new, it is born out of a potentiality sparked by Abraham's own desire (Zornberg, 1995).

Commentary on this passage in the Zohar cites kabbalist Chaim Vital: "Every person must search and discover the root of his soul so he can fulfill it and restore it to its source, its essence. The more one fulfills himself, the closer he approaches his authentic self" (Matt, 2004a, p. 9). Here, the yearning for transformation is equated with the soul's longing to return to its source in the divine, to be at-one with God. However, unlike other mystical traditions such as Buddhism, the moment of transformation in this state of union is, significantly, not a matter of the soul's negation but rather of its fulfillment—via authentic experience of self.

The third meaning of *teshuva,* response, is one that implies a relationship between two subjects. The desire for transformation is not one-sided—it is a mutual longing that spurs a loving interaction between the human being and God. Says the Zohar, "once one has aroused arousal, then arousal above is aroused" (Matt, 2004a, p. 7). The directive to Abraham does not, as it appears in simple translation of the Torah text, spring externally from God, from out of the blue. According to kabbalistic interpretation, Abraham's internal awakening arouses the divine call—God's command is given in *response* to Abraham's desire for enlargement and self-realization. In fact, it appears that it is just such a moment God has been waiting for all along.

Integrating Perspectives of Transformation

Although both psychoanalysis and religion have in common a concern with personal transformation, their relationship has historically been a conflicted one. William James demonstrated in *The Varieties of Religious Experience* (1902) that the study of spirituality and religious experience could open a door to understanding the nature of the self. Psychotherapy first flowered in the United States at the beginning of the 20th century under the auspices of the church-based Emmanuel Movement (Caplan, 1998). However, in order to establish its claim as a science, psychology considered it necessary to spurn the religious roots of psychotherapy: psychotherapy, and with it, the newly introduced technique of psychoanalysis, was subsumed under the purview of the medical profession. On the other side of the Atlantic, Jung's emphasis on spirituality and mysticism contributed to his split with Freud, who later labeled religion a "mass delusion" (Freud, 1927, p. 85).

Until only recently, it has been taboo to speak directly of religion or spirituality in connection with psychoanalytic process; in some orthodox psychoanalytic circles it is still ill advised to do so (Sorenson, 2004). Conversations between psychoanalysis and religion have often entailed each discipline trying to explain away the other, with psychoanalysis primarily emphasizing religion's defensive function and religion remaining wary of psychological reductionism. However, there appears to be a gradual rapprochement between the two fields as scholars of religion integrate psychoanalytic theory into their explication of religious or spiritual themes (Ostow, 1995, 2007; Zornberg, 1995, 2002) and psychoanalytic writers with religious and theological interests seek to foster a dialogue "in which religion and psychoanalysis meet in a profound space in which neither is statically master or slave, neither annexes or subsumes the other" (Sorenson, 2004, p. 39).

There is a growing interest among contemporary authors in a psychoanalytic understanding of spirituality and religious experience as well as integration of religious perspectives of transformation into considerations of psychic change (Aron, 2004; Eigen, 1998; Jones, 2002; Meissner & Schlauch, 2003; 2006; Sorenson, 2004; Spezzano and Gargiulo, 1997). Themes such as reverence, awe, surrender, and atonement, traditionally used to describe states of mystical experience, are frequently being used to describe what takes place in the psychoanalytic situation (Andresen, 1999; Benjamin, 1995; Davidson, 2001; Eigen, 1998; Ghent, 1990; Jones, 2002). The conceptualization of the dynamic of the analytic dyad has also shifted; whereas in the classical model, transformation takes place only in the patient, in the contemporary view, both parties are transformed via the relationship (Aron, 1996).

I am proposing here that a richer and more complete understanding of psychic change can be gained from an application to psychoanalytic process of the metaphors of transformation of religious experience in general, and as will be discussed more fully in the next chapter, those of Jewish mysticism in particular. Underlying this proposition is the position that the task of transformation in psychoanalysis involves not only coping with reality, but also transcending familiar modes of being—living in and appreciating the moment, knowing the self deeply, and entering into a new relationship, a truer and more meaningful one, with one's self, with others, and with the universe of which we are a part. These are also the strivings of spirituality, albeit undertaken through different means.

Ghent (2002) writes:

> Every day in our practice we pay homage to, and stand back in awe of, the marvels of the human mind caught up in the struggle to heal and transcend itself, while holding back in fear, jousting with itself in dread of walking through the valley of the shadow of death. (p. 808)

At some point in our lives, all of us, because we and those we love are human and therefore mortal, joust with dread. It is at these times that for some, a belief system offers not only comfort but also a way of moving through suffering to embrace life's heretofore-unseen possibilities. Faith is also a necessary component of the psychoanalytic endeavor: true psychic change inevitably requires a leap into the abyss of the unknown. Although formidable obstacles that stand in the way of change frequently confront both patient and analyst, both parties must have faith in the therapeutic process in order to acknowledge them, move through them, and thereby transcend them.

From the Scientific to the Sublime

The goals of psychoanalysis are inevitably shaped by the social and intellectual context of its times, as are its formulations of psychic change. Freud was eager to have psychoanalysis accepted as science and consistently emphasized the empirical basis of his theories, positioning his formulation of the workings of the human psyche as far as possible from the mythical and religious formulations of mankind that had preceded his theorizing. He dismissed the role of intuition in epistemology, describing the *Weltanschauung* of psychoanalysis, which he considered to be a branch of the sciences, as asserting "there are no sources of knowledge of the universe other than the intellectual working-over of carefully scrutinized observations—in other words, what we call research—and alongside of it no knowledge derived from revelation, intuition or divination" (p. 159). Intuition for Freud was illusion, the fulfillment of wishful impulse and an evasion of reality that was to be avoided. Freud went so far as to warn that inclusion of intuition into the sphere of knowledge would "lay open the paths which lead to psychosis" (p. 160).

Freud viewed religion as a product of humanity's need to defend itself against anxiety in the face of the brutal force of nature. In his treatment of the subject, he initially limited his study to religion's more rational aspects, acknowledging in his *Future of an Illusion* (1927), "I was concerned much less with the deepest sources of the religious feeling than with what the common man understands by his religion—with the system of doctrines and promises" (p. 74). However, in *Civilization and Its Discontents* (1930), Freud refers to his correspondence with Romain Rolland, in which Rolland objected that Freud had omitted in his treatise an examination of the fundamental element of religious experience, "a sensation of 'eternity,' the peculiar feeling … the feeling as of something limitless, unbounded—as it were, 'oceanic'" (p. 64), in other words, the prototypical mystical experience. Here Freud confesses that this phenomenon caused him "no small difficulty":

> I have nothing to suggest which could have a decisive influence on the solution of this problem. The idea of men's receiving an intimation of their connection with the world around them through an immediate feeling which is from the outset directed to that purpose sounds so strange and fits in so badly with the fabric of our psychology that one is justified in attempting to discover a psycho-analytic—that is, a genetic—explanation of such a feeling. (p. 65)

Freud likened the oceanic feeling to the state of being in love, a limitless narcissism, in which the boundary between ego and object "threaten to melt away" (p. 66). He proposed that at the beginning of life, the ego is all embracing, and includes both itself and the external world. Later, it carves itself out from the external world, but this original feeling-state survives alongside the more developed ego; "our present ego-feeling is, therefore, only a shrunken residue of a much more inclusive—indeed, an all-embracing—feeling which corresponded to a more intimate bond between the ego and the world about it" (p. 68). The oceanic feeling, Freud suggested, could be traced back to this earlier phase of development, to the infant-maternal bond. Although he maintained that the feeling of 'oneness with the universe' appeared to be "another way of disclaiming the danger which the ego recognizes as threatening it from the external world" (p. 72), the problem continued to cause him discomfort. He concludes by saying, "Let me admit once more that it is very difficult for me to work with these almost intangible quantities" (p. 72).

Freud's equation of the oceanic feeling with a state of primal, all-embracing inclusiveness resonates with more mystical formulations of at-one-ment, in particular, the kabbalistic idea that each individual soul is an aspect of God, longing to return to its source. According to the kabbalistic formulation, it is only as the result of *tzimtzum*, God's contraction of Himself, that we regard ourselves as having individual identities, separate and distinct selves. Although Freud himself was not convinced that he had satisfactorily explained the oceanic feeling of religious experience, psychoanalytic theorists for the most part have continued without question to attribute this expansive feeling of "being at-one-with" to the early infant-maternal relationship (see Ostow, 2007). Concomitantly, the individual's experience of this state, or his or her desire to reexperience it, has traditionally been viewed as a defensive or regressive phenomenon, rather than as the emotional achievement it would be considered to be in a spiritual context. Much has changed in the cultural clearing since the early days of psychoanalysis. The scientific climate in which classical psychoanalysis was embedded, characterized by faith in the rational, the observable, and the objective, has been knocked off its pedestal by Einstein's theory of relativity, quantum physics, and Heisenberg's "uncertainty principle." Mitchell (1993) says:

> Today's physicists spend much time revering the mysterious, and the modern scientific sensibility is less hard and sober than abstract and aesthetic. If today's science is a solution to the problem of

nihilism, it is a solution not aimed at a full, clear understanding and control but one of appreciation and awe. (p. 20)

Einstein (1993) himself writes:

The most beautiful experience we can have is the mysterious. It is the fundamental emotion that stands at the cradle of true art and true science. Whoever does not know it and can no longer wonder, no longer marvel, is as good as dead, and his eyes are dimmed. (p. 2)

There has been an accompanying paradigm shift in contemporary psychoanalysis toward an attitude of receptive curiosity and openness to mystery, as well as a sense of awe, states that are more familiarly evocative of religious experience. McWilliams (2004) writes:

The sense of awe is usually associated with ... the numinous realm, the place of the spirit. It is intrinsically connected with humility, the acknowledgment that human beings are, as Mark Twain observed, "the fly-speck of the universe" and that each of us is impelled by countless forces outside our own awareness and control. Awe involves the willingness to feel very small in the presence of the vast and unknowable. It is receptive, open to being moved. It bears witness. ... It is not antiscientific, but it defines scientific activity in much broader ways than the logical positivist who breaks huge, complex issues down into small and simple ones so that concepts can be easily operationalized and variables readily controlled. Awe allows our experience to take our breath away; it invites each client to make a fresh imprint on the soul, the psyche, of the therapist. (p. 32)

Andresen (1999) places within the feeling of awe a deeply felt respect for the transcendence of the other, "a new or recovered experiencing of the object's otherness or separateness from the subject," which "comes with the quality of a revelation" and "offers the opportunity for enlarging reflective self-awareness" (p. 507). Paradoxically, what Freud described as the melting away of boundaries may lead to heightened awareness of self and other, as Benjamin (1995) illustrates, drawing upon the imagery of Rilke's "awesome transforming angel" in her development of the themes of surrender and recognition in the erotic transference. "The flowing of the idealization out onto the analyst and the analytic space makes for Paradise, a space of self-discovery" (pp. 171–172).

Andre Green (1999) contrasts the work of the negative in psychoanalysis—its dealing with loss, absence, latent meaning—with the positivism of philosophy and objective discovery. "Psychoanalysis speaks of the opacity of another person's psyche which can *never be overcome* and is irreducible" (p. 15). Psychoanalysis, according to Green, must not seek to eliminate emotional experience by applying logic and abstract thinking, but instead must be able work with the *jouissance* of the emotional experience, the awesome, numinous, shattering pain or rapture of it. Like Jacob and his mysterious wrestling partner, the analytic dyad must be able "to keep the emotional experience in the mind and to reflect on it, to transform it without evacuating it, to be aware of it, without either being overwhelmed by it or by eliminating it" (Green, 1998, p. 365).

Creativity and Renewal and the Longing for Surrender

In Freud's civilized and repressive Vienna, where open expression of sexuality and aggression was deemed unacceptable, patients with symptoms of hysteria made up the majority of Freud's practice. In contrast, more and more, the pathology seen in those who appear in modern-day analysts' offices involves feelings of emptiness and lack of personal meaning in the experience of living (Cushman, 1995; Epstein, 1996; Mitchell, 1993). Concomitantly, the hope inspiring the analytic process is less the renunciation of illusion for the sake of rational knowledge and self-mastery and more the desire to create an authentic and enriching personal reality, and to expand the range of life's possibilities, including authentic connections with others based on feelings that are felt to be real and internally generated.

Freud's treatment of creativity, discovery, and spirituality came under criticism from his contemporaries, even from friendly quarters. Both Romain Rolland and Oskar Pfister, the Swiss Lutheran pastor who was Freud's lifelong friend and correspondent (Meng and Freud, 1963), argued with Freud that his treatment of religious experience in particular and transcendent experiencing in general limited the scope of psychoanalysis's ability to grasp the human situation. William James, also a contemporary of Freud's, echoed a similar sentiment regarding the limitations of psychology with regard to the transcendent aspects of human experience:

> One must have musical ears to know the value of a symphony; one must have been in love one's self to understand a lover's state of mind. Lacking the heart or the ear, we cannot interpret the musician or the lover justly, and we are even likely to consider him weak-minded or absurd. The mystic finds that most of us accord to his expectations an equally incompetent treatment. (1902, p. 300).

Contemporary psychoanalytic scholarship has paid increasing attention to humanity's spiritual and aesthetic yearnings, a shift that can be traced to Winnicott's (1967) reconsideration of cultural experience as an extension of transitional phenomena. Winnicott reframed illusion as a vehicle for attaining emotional maturity, as a way to *relate* to reality rather than to defend against it. He believed that the infant grows from a state of absolute dependence to a relative state of independence through her use of the "transitional object," with which the child relates her subjective reality, her internally generated truths, to a shared reality that can be objectively perceived by the external world. He posited that the capacity for illusion is a necessary step toward relationship with others. In his development of the concept of transitional experiencing, Winnicott linked illusion with creativity and insight, viewing it as a source of truth rather than as an evasion of reality that must be avoided.

Winnicott saw artistic creativity and religious feeling as manifestations of transitional experiencing, characterized by the growth-enhancing ability to enter into shared illusions, to relate inner and outer reality. Asking the question, "What is life about?" Winnicott concluded that what makes human life human and therefore worth living, is not merely instinctual satisfaction, but the richness of experience of the transitional realm. "The potential space between the baby and the mother, between the child and the family, between the individual and society or the world … can be looked upon as sacred to the individual in that it is here that the individual experiences creative living" (p. 372).

Winnicott extended the idea of a transitional space for creative play to include the analytic situation, in which the analyst might use the transference to understand what she is being used to do as well as whom she represents, and the analytic hour is used as a potential space for entering into collaborative exchange. The transformative possibilities inherent in areas of transitional experiencing, such as music, art, and religion, in which meaning from the inner world is infused into actions and objects in the public sphere, are potentiated in the analytic hour. Intuition as a basis of knowledge is not dismissed as a fulfillment of wishful impulse but is seen as a path to authentic experience and creative living.

Jones (2002) proffers Winnicott's theories as a framework for a psychoanalytic appreciation of the transformative capacities of religious experience. He writes:

> Religious experiences allow entrance again and again into that transforming psychological space from which renewal and creativity emerge. Rituals, words, stories, and introspective disciplines evoke those transitional psychological spaces, continually reverberating with the affects of past object relations and pregnant with the possibility of future forms of intuition and transformation. (p. 84)

Ghent (1990) also links the transformative possibilities of religion and psychoanalysis, referring to a "longing for surrender" of what Winnicott called the false self for the sake of authenticity, "the discovery of one's identity, one's sense of self, one's sense of wholeness, even one's sense of unity with other living beings" (p. 111). The sense of unity is, in Ghent's view, an emotional achievement, recognition of what we have in common as human beings. Surrendering to experience potentiates an encounter of the true self. Transformative rather than informational, being rather than knowing, surrender results in a feeling of spontaneity and aliveness, openness to experience, and the enhanced ability to relate to others from a position of authenticity. Ghent posits that surrender may be mutual—at least some analysts are motivated to pursue their profession by their own deeply rooted longings for surrender. "When the yearning for surrender is, or begins to be, realized by the analyst, the work is immensely fulfilling and the analyst grows with his patients" (p. 133).

Bollas (1987), too, places surrender at the heart of the process of transformation. For Bollas, the infant's early experiences are encoded not in object representations but in diffuse and affective sensations, the "shadow of the object." The infant's primal senses, the "unthought known," consist of bodily sensations, smells, sights, and sounds that are experienced within the relational matrix formed by the mother-child dyad. Bollas terms this primal maternal milieu the "transformational object" because within it, the child learns to transform her sensations into information about herself and the world. The infant, according to Bollas, experiences the mother as a *process* of transformation. The mother is the infant's "other self" but she is less an object than a way of being. The child is transformed through the mother's presence and care.

Bollas contends that the longing for transformation persists into adulthood, but "the quest is not to possess the object; rather the object is pursued in order to surrender to it as a medium that alters the self" (p. 14). Bollas traces the roots of faith and hope to the recollection of this preverbal, symbiotic ego memory. Religious or aesthetic moments that evoke the original experience of transformation inspire awe and reverence and assume the quality of the sacred, because they are part of the "unthought known," evocative of the baby's preverbal *being* in the presence of the transformational object. It is a "caesura in time when the subject feels held in symmetry and solitude by the spirit of the object" (p. 31), a wordless moment when one is felt to be transformed from a state of fragmentation to one of wholeness. One may be flooded with a profound sense of gratitude and a perception that the world has a sacred quality; this feeling is the shadow cast by the original transformational object during the stage of preverbal being, and that remains present throughout adulthood.

Bollas extends the idea of the transformational object to the analytic situation: "As the patient regresses into need, searching for a miraculous transformation, the analyst's ordinary work of listening, clarifying and interpreting introduces a different idiom of transforming psychic life" (p. 23). The reparative relationship with the analyst, rather than being the magical transformation the patient hopes for, is instead the "good-enough" transformational object relation, the envelopment by a benign maternal presence that the patient lacked at the beginning of life.

Loewald also roots the experience of the sacred in the *being* of the maternal-infant matrix. Although he considered himself to be an interpreter of Freudian theory, his might be considered a radical exegesis, mystical in its implications even while cloaked in orthodoxy (Jones, 2001). Loewald writes, "Freud was not a religious man and certainly not a mystic. But one does not have to be a mystic to remain open to the mysteries of life and human individuality, to the enigmas that remain beyond all the elucidations of scientific explanation and interpretations" (1978, p. 25). Loewald translates Freud's "*Wo Es war, soll Ich warden,*" as "where id was, there shall ego *come into being,*" holding that psychic transformation is a matter of the ego's renewal by the dynamic unconscious. The interplay between the dynamic unconscious and the ego, a reciprocal shaping of different levels of mentation, is what makes human life human. Irrational forces have the potential to enrich and transform the rational. Loewald uses the term "conscire," knowing together, to describe the intersection of unconscious with conscious knowing, explicitly connecting this form of knowing with mysticism. Deeply felt religious experience, because it arises from the id, has the potential to enrich and transform a civilization that has grown too rigidly rationalistic.

Inherent to the knowing of the unconscious is a sense of unity and timelessness, rooted in the infant-maternal relationship that exists before the development of ego boundaries, and before the capacity to make distinctions develops. Echoing Heidegger, Loewald terms this state "being." From this unitary state, mental processes differentiate, enabling a complex, mutual relationship among different levels of mentation, and potentiating "conscire," the knowing together. Like Freud, Loewald calls this state narcissism, a narcissism that "does not refer primarily to love of self in contrast to love of others, but to that primordial love-mentation which does not structure or divide reality into poles of inner and outer, subject and object, self and other" (1978, p. 42). With these words, Loewald is describing the prototypical mystical experience. The timelessness of the unconscious transcends the boundaries of temporal knowing. It is "structured or centered differently, that beginning, and ending, temporal succession and simultaneity, are not a part" of it (p. 68). Although these primary process states originate from the beginning of the infant's life, this does not mean that they must be discarded—to the contrary, their presence throughout adulthood is vital to being fully alive.

Loewald's vision of a rich human life, and by extension, a successful analytic product, is like Winnicott's, a sense of aliveness and openness to experience without which the human condition would be desolate. He writes:

> It would seem that the more alive people are ... the broader their range of ego-reality levels is. Perhaps the so-called fully developed, mature ego is not one that has become fixated at the presumably highest or latest stage of development, having left the others behind it, but is an ego that integrates its reality in such a way that the earlier and deeper levels of ego-reality integration remain alive as dynamic sources of higher organization. (p. 20)

and

> The range and richness of human life is directly proportional to the mutual responsiveness between these various mental phases and levels ... While [objective rationality is] a later development, it limits and impoverishes ... the perspective, understanding, and range of human action, feeling, and thought, unless it is brought back into coordination and communication with those modes of experience that remain their living source, and perhaps their ultimate destination. It is not a foregone conclusion that man's objectifying mentation is, or should be, an ultimate end rather than a component and intermediate phase ... (Loewald, 1978, p. 61)

Beyond Memory and Desire: From Knowing to Becoming

Well aware of the disturbing impact that it would have on what he called the Psychoanalytic Establishment, Wilfred Bion introduced explicitly mystical ideas into his theoretical formulations of psychoanalytic process and clinical practice. He questioned the idea of science as being limited to objective discovery, insisting that psychoanalysis, mysticism, and scientific discovery all had in common the seeker's "at-one-ment" with ultimate reality or absolute truth, the truth of an object that could never be known but whose presence could be intuited.

"In his mother's womb man knows the universe and forgets it at birth" writes Bion (1977a, p. 13), citing the Jewish myth rooted in kabbalistic teaching recounted by Martin Buber in *I and Thou* (1923, p. 76).

In his effort to conceptualize the roots of psychic activity, Bion spent his lifetime on the quest to regain a portion of that lost knowledge. Based on his experience with psychotic patients, he drew upon the mother-infant relationship in establishing his criteria of a good psychoanalytic session. Bion believed that the mother nourishes her infant not only by feeding but also by her reverie about her child—through registering its experience, feeling compassion and understanding when it is distressed, and communicating this to her baby through her voice and her actions. Through this process, the infant develops the capacity to think; if the process fails, the infant is left with nonsymbolized experience, beta elements that are felt as persecutory "things-in themselves." Bion viewed the reverie of the analyst as critical to facilitating the patient's ability to think, what he termed the transformation of beta elements into alpha function, or the ability to establish links leading to the awareness of constant conjunctions that can be named.

At the heart of the question of what is transformative in psycho-analytic process is the enigma of how the patient moves from insight to change, from intellectual understanding to a newly felt way of being. Bion (1977b) phrased the issue as "how to pass from 'knowing' 'phenomena' to 'being' that which is 'real'" and, more clearly, "Is it possible through psycho-analytic interpretation to effect a transition from knowing the phenomena of the real self to being the real self?" (p. 148). He conceived of the sign 'O' to designate absolute truth and ultimate reality, encompassing both good and evil; from a mathematical vertex, the infinite; and from a religious vertex, the godhead. Transformation involves "being" rather than "knowing" and entails "being in O," at one with the truth of the psychoanalytic session. Bion's term for knowing is 'K,' a prerequisite for "being in O" but not sufficient for it: "Any interpretation may be accepted in K but rejected in O; acceptance in O means that acceptance of an interpretation enabling the patient to 'know' that part of himself to which attention has been drawn is felt to involve 'being' or 'becoming' that person" (p. 164). Resistance is resistance to the transformation from K → O; the transformation to O requires the taking of responsibility by the patient, growth in emotional maturity; it is feared because accepting responsibility requires feeling pain. Bion speaks of the diameter of an interpretation needing to be not too small and not too large. Telling a patient what he already knows is not useful (the diameter is too small); making too abstruse an interpretation relates to the desire in the analyst to see farther than the patient (the diameter is too large). An interpretation is ripe for the making when it is apparent to the analyst that resistance is operating not only in the patient but also in himself—the analyst feels a resistance in himself to the reaction of the patient if the interpretation were made.

For Bion, the beginning of a session encompasses the formulation of the godhead, or ultimate reality. From there, a pattern emerges, with which the analyst seeks to establish contact with O and then make his interpretation. O is not attainable through K (represented by Bion as K→O); but in transformation O→K, at-one-ment with O is made possible by ridding K of memory and desire. The state of mind required to apprehend O is what Bion calls "faith," faith in ultimate reality and the ultimate truth of the session. Being at-one with O is an ineffable experience. Faith entails being receptive to O; ridding oneself of memory and desire makes possible the awareness of phenomena that are evolutions of O, which can be perceived through sensuously derived mental functions. Bion offers no rules for interpretation, only rules for the analyst to help him "achieve the frame of mind in which he is receptive to O of the analytic experience" (1977c, p. 32). Being receptive to O requires an act of faith.

In both psychoanalysis and science, contends Bion, the relationship between acts of faith to thought is analogous to the relationship of *a priori* knowledge to knowledge. "It must 'evolve' before it can be apprehended and it is apprehended when it is a thought" (p. 35). It has no relation to sensation or to memory and desire. Yet, " ... no one who denudes himself of memory and desire, and of all those elements of sense impression ordinarily present, can have any doubt of the reality of the psychoanalytical experience which remains ineffable" (p. 35). Bion compares Freud's self-described method of "blinding himself artificially" when working with a particularly obscure problem, with eschewing memory and desire but extends this state of artificial blindness to include the suspension of rational understanding and sense impressions. This is not, Bion maintains, a denial of reality, but rather the path to achieving contact with O, or psychic reality. "The analyst has to *become infinite* by the suspension of memory, desire, understanding" (p. 46).

Bion cautions that this experience can be a disturbing one, producing a feeling of dread. In the process of ridding oneself of memory and desire, painful emotions that had been previously disguised may emerge, even if the analyst has himself undergone analysis. Psychic change or maturation requires an "abandonment of control over the proportion of pain to plea-sure and leaves it to forces that are outside the personality. At-one-ment or unity with O is in prospect fearful" (p. 53). The analyst, by freeing him-self of memory and desire, will be able to approximate the state of being left only with his invariants, the functions that make up his "irreducible, ultimate man. ... Upon his ability to approximate to this will depend his ability to achieve the 'blindness' that is a prerequisite for 'seeing' the evolved elements of O" (p. 58). In turn, this ability will enable to him to 'see' the analysand's invariant aspects of O. "The further the analysis progresses the more the psycho-analyst and the analysand achieve a state in which both contemplate the irreducible minimum that is the patient" (p. 59).

Whereas Freud discounted intuition as a basis of knowledge, Bion places intuition center-stage. His prescription for psychoanalysts to rid themselves of memory and desire is given in order to clear a space for *intuiting* the evolution of a session. By being attuned not to what has happened or what will happen, but what is currently happening in the moment, the analyst will be able to build "his psychoanalytic technique on a firm basis of intuiting evolution and NOT on the shifting sand of slight experience imperfectly remembered" (2005, p. 382). Quoting Keats, Bion advocates an attitude where "a man is capable of being in uncertainties, mysteries, doubts without any irritable reaching after fact and reason" (cited in Bion, 1977c, p. 125). Regarding the aims of analysis, Bion does not claim to reach beyond approximation, recognizing that to some extent, knowledge inherently necessitates a loss of absolute truth in comparison with the formless infinite. He defines the goal of the analytic process in words that could have been spoken by a kabbalist articulating the cosmic processes put into effect by personal transformation:

> What is to be sought is an activity that is both the restoration of god (the Mother) and the evolution of god (the formless, infinite, ineffable, non-existent), which can be found only in the state in which there is NO memory, desire, understanding. (p. 129)

A More Permeable Boundary

In the beginning, Freud championed positivism, rationality, and objec-tive discovery as being the foundations of psychoanalytic knowledge.

Later theorists felt it necessary to find a place for the nonrational in formulations that attempted to explain the mystery of psychic enlargement and renewal. It is apparent that, given the numerous transformations that psychoanalytic theory has itself undergone over time, psychoanalytic and religious formulations of transformation are not as far apart as they once seemed, or as Freud would have preferred to believe. The creation of a space within psychoanalytic theory for an appreciation of the transformative possibilities of aesthetic and creative experiencing and for intuition as a source of truth makes the boundary between religion and psychoanalysis a more permeable one, allowing for a potentially fruitful collaborative exchange.

Central to the paradigm shift in psychoanalytic thought is an increasing concern with how meaning is created in the context of human relatedness. Mitchell (2000) highlights in particular, the significance of Loewald's theoretical contributions in radically transforming the basic values that guide the psychoanalytic undertaking and in shaping contemporary relational theorizing. In calling for the revitalization of the link between fantasy and reality, primary and secondary process, the primal dense unity of "being" with the differentiated experience of self, Loewald places meaning, imagination, and aliveness at the heart of the psychoanalytic enterprise. Rather than the triumph of the rational over the irrational, the goal of the analytic project becomes the ability to move fluidly from one realm of experience to the other.

Within the framework of the analytic relationship, the at-one-ment of the mother-child matrix is evoked as a medium through which the present is transformed and new meanings are generated. In turn, the lived reality of the transference-countertransference interaction brings to life the ghosts of the past, and through the interpretive understanding of both participants, makes possible their transformation into ancestors that enrich and enliven the present. Implicit in both Loewald's vision of therapeutic action and the kabbalistic notion of *teshuva* is the capacity of the individual to transcend the boundaries of time, to change the significance of the past in the context of the here-and-now, and to do so within the mutative field of relationship. Loewald writes, "It is thus not only true that the present is influenced by the past, but also that the past—as a living force within the patient—is influenced by the present" (Loewald, 1974, cited in Mitchell, 2000, p. 49).

Drawing on Loewald's vision of mind as embedded, from the beginning, in an interactive field with other minds, and further developing from these interactions, Mitchell proposes a system of mutual influence between the individual and the larger relational matrix, in which each, the microcosm and the macrocosm, shape and transform one another:

In the beginning ... is the relational ... matrix in which we discover ourselves. ... Within that matrix are formed ... individual psyches with subjectively experienced interior spaces. Those subjective spaces begin as microcosms of the relational field, in which macrocosmic interpersonal relationships are internalized and transformed into a distinctly personal experience; and those personal experiences are, in turn, regulated and transformed, generating newly emergent properties, which in turn create new interpersonal forms that alter macrocosmic patterns of interaction. Interpersonal relational processes generate intrapsychic relational processes which reshape interpersonal processes reshaping intrapsychic processes, on and on in an endless Mobius strip in which internal and external are perpetually regenerating and transforming themselves and each other. (p. 57)

I believe that Mitchell is expressing here in psychological terms what the kabbalists articulated on the spiritual plane, projecting their vision further outward into the cosmos: namely, that there exists a relationship of reciprocal influence between the microcosm and the macrocosm, between the individual and the larger whole of which he is an inextricable part. Furthermore, as Mitchell suggests, and as the kabbalists intuited in their development of their theosophical and sefirotic systems, there exist modes of organization that vary according to degrees of articulation of spatial, temporal, and perceptual boundaries. The specific world of reality that we perceive in our everyday lives is the sum of an infinitely complex interaction, back and forth among these different dimensions of being. Although one may feature more prominently in the foreground of conscious awareness at any given time, they each exist, and continue to operate, in dialectical and dynamic relationship with one another. In both psychoanalytic and kabbalistic formulations of transformation, living a life of vitality and meaning requires moving fluidly among these varying domains of experience, and cultivating the life-sustaining channels of mutual influence between the primal dense unity of being and the demarcated boundaries of individual existence.

4. The Interpretive Encounter

Rabbi Bunam said: It is written in Proverbs: "As in water face answers to face, so the heart of man to man." Why does the verse read "in water" and not "in a mirror"? Man can see his reflection in water only when he bends close to it, and the heart of man too must lean down to the heart of his fellow; then it will see itself within his heart. (Buber, 1947, p. 263)

The Journey of the Soul

Written in a combination of Aramaic and Hebrew, the Zohar, or Book of Splendor, is the main body of medieval kabbalistic teachings. It is a resplendent assemblage of Jewish myth, mysticism, and esotericism. Revealed in bits and pieces at the end of the 13th century by a group of Castilian kabbalists who claimed they had discovered the teachings of 2nd-century Rabbi Shimon Bar Yochai, the Zohar is believed by modern scholars to have been written by Moses de Leon, the man at the center of this Castilian kabbalistic circle, with possible contributions by some of his associates. The act of committing to writing what was previously oral tradition is thought to be partly a reaction against the rationalism of the Jewish philosopher Maimonides as well as an attempt to revitalize a Judaism that had become overly intellectualized and distant from human concerns (Green, 2004). The Zohar was written in the context of the "cosmic spirituality" of the Middle Ages, in which the epistemologies of science, philosophy, and religion were considered parts of a unified whole, and "essential to the quest for wisdom or truth" (Green, 2004, p. 102). In their cosmogony, the kabbalists embraced the challenge of reconciling the abstract God of the philosophers with the personal God of the Jewish Bible and myth.

At the same time, the Zohar is intently concerned with the psychological and spiritual life of the individual, as represented by the soul and its struggle for balance, both internally and in relation to the external world. Its insistence on attending closely to the unconscious and preconscious aspects of human existence prompts its characterization, as that of psychoanalysis, as "a critique of the status quo and of conventional society" (Rosenberg, 2000, p. 25). The Zohar's literary method has likewise been compared with the psychoanalytic method. "Both peel away the layers of defense against an insight by a method of indirection, one that is always on the lookout for a clue to either the interior life of the soul or the unconscious" (p. 169). Just as psychoanalysis cannot be said to have one definitive "cure" as its aim, there is not one specific goal at the heart of the Zohar's way of reading, only the encouragement of the individual on his journey toward self-awareness.

There are, of course, fundamental differences between the Kabbalah and psychoanalysis. Most notably, the word "analysis" means the separation of things into constituent parts or elements, whereas the mystic mind tends to hold the world together, to see all things as one. But like the psychoanalyst, the kabbalist strives "to behold the seen in conjunction with the unseen, to keep the fellowship with the unknown through the revolving door of the known" (Heschel, 1996, p. 165). This chapter examines the Kabbalah's metaphors of transformation as they relate to the interpretive encounter, demonstrating the centrality of relationship in the Kabbalah's interpretive process, and creating a dialogue with contemporary psychoanalytic views of interpretation.

Seeking Truth through Language

Definitively rooted in the *halachic* and interpretive tradition of rabbinic Judaism, the Zohar displays a "heightened midrashic sensitivity," keenly attuned to the latent meanings of the Torah text (Green, 2004). The root of the word *midrash* means, "to seek out" or "inquire," implying attentiveness to facets of meaning that are not immediately apparent on first reading. From a psychoanalytic point of view, the *peshat,* or simple reading of the text, can be considered to be its conscious meaning, while *midrash* comprises the "unconscious … encrypted traces of more complex meaning" (Zornberg, 2002, p. 3). In their hermeneutic practice, the kabbalists liberally employ the midrashic structure, but then go beyond it, posing questions that hint at further significance. Some kabbalistic texts refer to mystical interpretations as the "soul" of the Torah, while its legalistic derivations are called the "body," and its narrative the "garments." The body and garments, comprising the manifest layer of the Torah's language, paradoxically serve dual and opposing purposes: they veil what is hidden, and give form to that which has no form, making its perception possible.

Language is perceived by the kabbalists as spanning all of truth, and thus as a fitting medium through which truth may be discerned. The Zohar notes that the three consonants of the Hebrew word for truth— *emet*—*aleph, mem,* and *tav,* are the first, middle, and last letters of the Hebrew alphabet: truth stretches from the beginning to end of language. Linguistic elements, together with the *sefirot,* form the building blocks of the universe. The idea of language as a foundational creative structure is evocative of Lacan's interpretation of Freud's fundamental insight, that "the unconscious is structured in the most radical way like a language" (1977, p. 234). For Lacan, the truth of the unconscious, although veiled, is revealed through language, through the discourse of the Other as it speaks to the analyst:

> Lacan associates the advent of the Symbolic with language. … The Imaginary tries to use or manipulate language so as to reinforce the subject's tyrannical illusion of mastery, his omnipotent self-encapsulation. The Symbolic provides a way out of self-enclosure through the subject's surrender to the life of meaning, the play of language, and the emergence of effective insights which outstrip his control. The gap between what is hidden and the pulsation of insight is respected and worked with, rather than delusively escaped or filled in. The subject is genuinely recreated through his participation in the movement of language, through his interaction with the Other, bearer of the Word (namely revelation). (Eigen, 1981, p. 419)

Both the kabbalist and the analyst, respecting the gap between the veiled and the unknown, attend closely to the nuances of language in their effort to perceive truth that is not superficially apparent and that speaks from its desire to be recognized. "'Truth' in its deepest sense, must encompass life; that is it must stir man's soul and perhaps even transform him in the process" (Drob, 2000a, p. 55). Both the kabbalist, and ideally, the analyst, use language to perceive truth that stirs the soul.

Although the text of the Zohar is presented as a commentary on the Torah, its interpretations of biblical verse evoke visual images that depict unseen realities—worlds within worlds, fluid creative processes, and relationships in dynamic tension—that can be observed only with the inner eye. For the kabbalists, all things exist in intimate and symbiotic relationship, a perception they articulate through the symbolism of the *sefirot*. The language of the Zohar is permeated with this symbolism, depicting the inner world of the soul as the mystics experienced it through reflective self-awareness and which they projected outward onto the cosmos. Hence, the language of sefirotic symbolism allowed not only for a manner of reading the Torah but also served as a paradigm with which to articulate the experience of personally entering into the realm of the *sefirot* through meditative contemplation (Green, 2004).

The kabbalists viewed their self-reflective exploration of their own inner worlds as an ascent to the heights of human capacity, a reaching out toward awareness of and connection with something larger than themselves. They understood the *sefirot* as aspects of God "clothed in garments"—paradoxically, both hidden and revealed—and so perceivable by the finite human mind. Through their meditative practices, the kabbalists brought forth the *sefirot* as reflecting mirrors with which to catch the divine light that they believed would otherwise overwhelm human perception. Therefore, to most fully appreciate the Zohar, one must read it not only as a creative commentary on a canonical text but also as an expression of the dynamics of the experienced inner life of the kabbalist (Idel, 2002).

Transformation through Interpretation

Interpretation in the Zohar is considered to be not an intellectual hermeneutical exercise, but a key to unlocking meanings both cosmic and personal. Each word, even letter, of the Torah is believed to enclose a spiritual significance whose depths may be fruitfully plumbed by the attentive interpreter. The characters of the Zohar are said to "open" with an interpretation, which in Talmudic parlance usually means to begin a back-and-forth, often legalistic, discussion, but in the Zohar, they literally open up the text to reveal a flowering penumbra of associations and a multiplicity of meanings that are described as enflaming the soul. To do so, they make use of associative links, numbers, and wordplay involving the spoken and written representations of words. The *process* of interpretation, not its result, is called *sod*, secret. There is not one secret to be uncovered but, rather, a method of reading that makes endless discoveries possible.

Unlike most spiritual or cosmic systems, in which it is assumed that there is one faithful interpretation of the text, the Kabbalah assumes the possibility of an infinite number of possible interpretations, attributable to the infinite nature of God (Idel, 2002). The Torah is considered to be a manifestation of the divine, the blueprint of the universe, and its continued sustaining and recreating presence. However, it requires engagement—it requires *relationship*—for its own sustenance and cosmic balance. Writes Idel, "This is not ... a static presence but one that depends on ... the people of Israel, who indeed are presented here as the people of the book—not a book that is imposed on them and venerated in servitude but one whose components are sustained by their acts" (p. 133). As the Torah is written in Hebrew, without vowels, it is a text that is particularly well suited for providing an infinite number of interpretations. Simply changing the pronounced vowels but leaving the text as written may completely change the meaning of a word or phrase. The kabbalists often played with this aspect of the Torah's language in their attempts to uncover hidden meanings.

The metaphor of play applies equally as well to the rabbinic interpretive tradition in which the Kabbalah is based. Zornberg (2002) writes of the Torah as a plaything bestowed by God, referring to Winnicott's concept of play as allowing for the experiences of union and difference with the other, in the space that lies between them. God depends on His people to play with the Torah, to interpret its verses, to experience themselves as separate from Him, and also as one with him. Zornberg likens the play of the Torah's language to the play of the language of poetry, which plays in the space of Keats's negative capability. To play with language, one must be capable of remaining in "uncertainty, mystery, and doubt." The play of poetry and of Torah, "arises at moments of transition, even of fracture of received narratives; old ways of combining words recede to the margins" (p. 391).

The kabbalists believed that their play with the language of the Torah held the power of continued creation, a strength that has similarly been attributed to the playfulness of poets:

> [It] is the product of their shared ability to appreciate the power of re-describing, the power of language to make new and different things possible and important—an appreciation which becomes possible only when one's aim becomes an expanding repertoire of alternative descriptions rather than The One Right Description. (Rorty, cited in Zornberg, 2002, p. 392)

The Kabbalah also plays in the literal space between the Torah's letters. Some kabbalistic writings associate the white parts of the Torah text (traditionally written by hand, using a quill pen and black ink on parchment) with the higher or inner level of the divine realm, describing it as the soul of the text that sustains the body, which is represented by the black letters (Idel, 2002). In some late-13th-century kabbalistic texts, the finite, limited, black letters are associated with the public and communal manifestation of the divine in the external world, which is necessarily finite. The spaces between the letters are linked with the formlessness and ambiguity of the highest levels of the divine, and are posited as the space of meeting between God and the human being. This in-between area is where encounter of the Other is possible, a transitional area of experiencing that both sharpens and transcends the boundaries of "me" and "not-me." Mutative interpretation, creating change in *both* God and the human being, occurs in this transitional space of meeting. This transitional space in which God and the human being encounter each other is referred to as the area of faith, an idea that will be further developed in the next chapter, along with its implications for psychoanalytic work.

The kabbalists perceived in the interpretive process transformational and dynamic qualities affecting both text and interpreter. A particular interpretation may depend on a synchronicity of inner and outer events. Isaac Luria ascribed to the Zohar itself an inexhaustible plentitude of meaning, maintaining that because the worlds are ever changing, the Zohar's aspects of meaning change, depending on the unique moment in time. He also held that different meanings are illuminated according to the developmental, experiential, and spiritual state of the particular interpreter. Positing an active transformation of the text through interpretation, the kabbalist Azulai believed that each time one reads a given verse of Torah, the combination of its linguistic elements change in response to the call of the moment (Drob, 2000a).

In vivid imagery, the Zohar depicts interpretation as a matter of mutual engagement between text and interpreter, two subjects who are each transformed by the encounter. The Torah in the Zohar is conceived as a living divine presence, participating in a mutual relationship with those who study her. (In Hebrew, the word "Torah" is feminine, and therefore the Torah is referred to as "she;" the kabbalists elaborated on this feature by describing the Torah in their metaphors using feminine imagery.) The interpretive relationship is portrayed as one of mutual arousal. Engagement with the Torah is compared with a lover's courtship of a maiden who is hidden in a palace, desiring to be revealed:

> Arousal within Torah is like an endless courting of the beloved: constant walking about the gates of her palace, an increasing passion to read her letters, the desire to see the beloved's face, to reveal her, and to be joined with her. The beloved in the nexus of this relationship is entirely active. She sends signals of her interest to her lover, she intensifies his passionate desire for her by games of revealing and hiding. She discloses secrets that stir his curiosity. She desires to be loved. The beloved is disclosed in an erotic progression before her lover out of a desire to reveal secrets that have been forever hidden within her. The relationship between Torah and her lover, like that of man and maiden in this parable, is dynamic, romantic, and erotic. This interpretive axiom of the work, according to which the relationship between student and that studied is not one of subject and object but of subject and subject ... opens up a great number of new possibilities ... (Hellner-Eshed, cited in Green, 2004, p. 69)

The Torah is not an object but a subject who longs for her innermost depths to be known. To know her requires a heightened subjectivity, a keen sensitivity to the veiled unknown, the "attentiveness that is the natural prayer of the soul" (Felstiner, 1995, p. xvii). To grow attentive to her subtext is to activate her verses. Their truth is sometimes obscure or ambiguous, but also fleetingly radiant. One emerges from the encounter enriched, having quickened dimensions of the self that are not ordinarily accessible to conscious awareness.

Later kabbalists, such as Rabbi Moses Chaim Luzzatto, further developed the theme of the mutuality of interpretation, likening the process to blowing on a hot coal whose flame is hidden, "but when you blow on it, it expands and broadens like a flame and many sorts of nuances are seen which were not visible prior to it in the coal, but everything emerged from the coal ... it is necessary to enflame it and then it will be enflamed, and so too the intellect of man" (cited in Idel, 2002, p. 97). The flame is a manifestation of what is latent in the coal, which can be illuminated only through the active participation of another in mutual relationship.

The image of the flame is often used by the kabbalists to describe the encounter with God. When flame is joined to flame, the two separate flames become one; although the individual perceives himself as a separate flame, or unique self, in the state of at-one-ment he recognizes that his existence is only a corporeal manifestation of a greater unity. The flame is also used as a metaphor for the human condition—the lowermost area of the flame is inexorably dependent on the wick, just as the *nefesh*, the animating soul, is dependent on the body; the middle part of the flame symbolizes *ruach*, the second level of the soul; the upper part of the flame symbolizes *neshama*, the third level of the soul which has its roots in the divine, and strives to rise ever higher toward its source.

Interpretation, too, is seen as a matter of striving upward, toward the soul's source in God. The kabbalists envisioned an intimate connection between the individual soul and its particular interpretation. Isaac Luria's disciple, Chaim Vital, wrote that every evening, Luria gazed on the faces of his disciples and saw a scriptural verse illuminated on the forehead.

The visualized verse was one that pertained to that particular student's soul, in accordance with the Lurianic notion that every soul possesses interpretations of Scripture that are unique to it. Luria would then partially explain the esoteric meaning of the verse in terms of the significance that it held for that individual's spiritual condition. The disciple was then instructed to concentrate upon the explanation he had been given and to recite the verse before going to sleep. He did this so that when his soul ascended to the upper realm during sleep, he might gain full knowledge of the verse's meaning. In this way, the individual's soul would increase in purity and ascend to still higher levels in the divine realm, where it would enjoy the revelation of additional mysteries of the Torah (Fine, 2003, p. 163).

According to some formulations of Lurianic writings, the soul's very essence is the expression of its interpretation. This expression is clearly a matter of *being* rather than intellectual *knowing*. "Faithful interpretation ... is conceived not so much as the projection of the values of the religious society onto an antiquated canon ... but as faithfulness to the inner nature of one's soul" (Idel, 2002, p. 98). In other words, the soul makes its unique and indispensable contribution to the universal through its interpretation.

Unlike the more familiar Western notion of exalting individual uniqueness, the contribution of a particular soul, or its divine spark, is considered not in isolation, but within the larger context of community. The individual is only one piece of a larger puzzle, yet essential to the greater whole. Each interpreter "reflects in himself the whole range of his community, just as his own interpretation, unique as it is, comprises in some mysterious way the whole spectrum of interpretations preserved within his community" (p. 99). The individual soul's interpretation enables the completion of the others', fostering a spirit of cooperation rather than the veneration of the individual. It is valued for its authenticity rather than its originality or creativity.

Interpretation's transformational effects are explicit. By being true to the roots of one's soul, one enables the expansion of the text and of one's self, and according to Lurianic doctrine, the restoration of the divine sparks to their source in the process of *tikkun* on both a cosmic and personal level. *Tikkun* holds that the relationship between God and humanity is one that is *mutually* sustaining—the heavenly and human planes affect each other in a bidirectional flow of influence and life-sustaining plenitude. As mentioned previously, the *sefirot* are not static but dynamic, and change in accordance with human actions. Hence, the rather startling proposition that humanity has the unique ability to affect the higher worlds through its actions in the lower world, to perfect the divine relationships (as represented by the *sefirot*) or to sever them. Cosmic and social *tikkun* is, in effect, set into motion through personal *tikkun*. And so, the individual act of interpretation within the context of the larger community—interpreted by Luria as being true to the roots of one's soul—has wider transformational implications than mere change within the individual or human society: by participating in the interpretive encounter, God, too, is transformed.

Psychoanalytic Interpretation

There is clearly an affinity between the kabbalistic and psychoanalytic valuation of language and their use of the interpretive process in the pursuit of individual self-awareness. Both disciplines attempt to discern reality not directly observable through sensory experience. Freud's (1900) detailed description of the method of arriving at the unconscious meaning of dream images is strikingly similar to the kabbalists' use of wordplay, associative links, and numerology in their interpretation of biblical verses. Interestingly, the kabbalists believed that, during sleep, the soul ascends to the roots of its interpretation (Idel, 2002), to the source of its being, which is outside of conscious awareness. In *The Interpretation of Dreams* (1900), Freud vividly describes his personal struggle for self-knowledge, showing in great detail "how the soul could become aware of itself" (Bettelheim, 1984, p. 4). Freud's method of interpreting dreams combines the use of the dreamer's associations as well as the symbols of the dream, whose meanings depend on the particular context in which the dream and the dreamer are embedded. The analyst's collaboration is with the patient's free associations. In Freud's view, the object of the analyst's interpretive method, whether in the interpretation of dreams or the patient's discourse, is to detect the true significance disguised by the patient's material, and to present it to the patient when the moment is ripe. Thus, the patient can be shown the pathway toward which to direct his energies, with the aim of cure.

The kabbalists, too, make use of symbols and associative links, a technique they refer to as jumping and skipping, in their interpretive method; but they emphasize that rather than one correct interpretation, many correct interpretations are possible, each of which may illuminate a hitherto unknown or unarticulated truth. In their treatment of the mutative capacity of interpretation, in other words, its ability to effect transformation, the kabbalists propose a mutuality that does not exist in Freud's formulation, but that appears in the work of later psychoanalytic theorists. In the kabbalists' framework, both interpreter and text contribute their own subjectivity to the encounter and each is transformed in the process. The kabbalists speak of the interpretive dyad as a relationship between two subjects, and of the interpretive process as engagement in a responsive interplay of recognition and concealment.

The images of enflaming and arousal, images used to describe interpretation's mutative capacity, are predicated on relationship. These metaphors suggest a sense of enlargement and enhanced awareness in *both* participants, engendered by the experience of knowing and being known, of seeking and being sought. Interpretation in kabbalistic terms is an endeavor that seeks expanded awareness of the self through reaching toward the soul's supernal root, which is ultimately beyond human knowledge. In turn, this very reaching out affects and transforms God Himself, restoring cosmic balance (Tishby, 1994).

The notion of a soul's expression as *being* its interpretation suggests a definition of interpretation very different from the classic psychoanalytic use of interpretation as *bedeutung,* "assigning meaning," and much closer to Bion's "'being' O" (1977b, p. 149). The authenticity of the soul can be thought of variously as its emotional truth, its unique and irreproducible essence, its particular divine spark, its peculiar specificity in being O, its manifestation of, and at-one-ment with, ultimate reality. Although the ultimate reality of the self is beyond the grasp of reason, it can, and must, be intuited, and thereby aroused, in order for change to occur. Reciprocally, the particular interpreter—that soul and no other—activates a particular aspect of meaning at one particular moment in time, and no other. Who is transforming whom? Arousal—transformation—occurs in both parties. Interpretation is "won from the void and formless infinite" (Bion, 1977b, p. 151) *at the point of meeting,* and both interpreter and the interpreted are transformed.

The mutative interpretation has been a traditional concern of psychoanalysis, as has consideration of the right moment for a particular interpretation (Pine, 1984): "The 'right' moment is often characterized by a certain affectivity—a surfacing and aliveness of conflict—that

heightens the likelihood that the analyst's words will have impact, trig-
gering further affect and productive thought processes" (p. 56). In the
classical model, interpretation is a one-way affair: only the patient is
affected. The analyst remains veiled, inscrutable, and unknowable.

The metaphor of the analyst as reflecting mirror, a neutral piece of
glass that permits only unidirectional reflection, pervades the classical
psychoanalytic literature. In contrast, as noted in the verse that begins
this chapter, the kabbalists prefer water as a metaphor for self-reflection
within the context of relationship: "Man can see his reflection in water
only when he bends close to it, and the heart of man too must lean down
to the heart of his fellow; then it will see itself within his heart" (Buber,
1947, p. 264). Water has dimension; although it reflects, it also reveals. If
one looks closely enough, one can see not only one's reflection, but also
the depths that lie beneath the surface. Similarly, in the analytic situation, an appreciation of the other's subjectivity is necessary in order for
one's own self-reflection to have dimension. The nature of water is that it
is continuously changing—as it ripples and flows, one's reflection ripples
and flows correspondingly. So, too, in the analytic dyad, one's reflection
is transformed as a function of the shifting subjectivity of the other.

Interpretation in the Context of Relationship

Since Freud's time, more contemporary psychoanalysts offer perspectives on interpretation that are nearer to the kabbalistic model of
mutuality. In these formulations, the subjectivity of the analyst figures,
to varying extents, in the transformational nature of interpretation.
Lacan (1977), interpreting Freud, locates the compulsion to repeat in
"the desire for recognition" that "dominates the desire that is to be
recognized, preserving it as such until it is recognized" (p. 133). The
analyst's role is to recognize the truth expressed by the discourse of the
unconscious; in other words, to discern the meaning of the metaphor
of the symptom. The analyst can do so when the truth resonates within
his own subjectivity as truth. By recognizing it subjectively as truth,
the analyst can then return it to the patient as the patient's truth. Thus
the patient dually benefits—not only by recognizing his own truth but
also by it having been recognized by another. Winnicott (1960), stress-
ing the importance of the analyst's willingness to tolerate *not knowing,*

speaks of interpretation as a way for the patient to become aware of the analyst's limitations, a realization that is crucial to the patient's developmental growth.

Ogden (1979) illustrates how, through projective identification, the processing of the patient's projected feelings by the analyst, and their subsequent return to the patient in a modified form, may facilitate psychic change in the patient. In the process, something new is created between them. In a more explicit use of the analyst's subjective states in interpretation, Bollas (1987) demonstrates the value, in certain cases, of the expression of the analyst's subjectivity. By indirectly making the analyst's subjective states available to the patient, the analyst "facilitates the articulation of heretofore inarticulate psychic life" (p. 210); in other words, articulation of the "unthought known," aspects of the patient's unconscious that are experienced but have never been verbalized. In the clinical examples that Bollas provides, it is apparent that his tone when offering his subjective states to the patient for consideration is musingly tentative and sometimes playful, making clear that his interpretations are not declarations of absolute truth, but offerings of possible truth that the patient is free to accept or reject, depending on their resonance with some unspoken aspect of his unconscious.

Following the British Independent Group analysts such as Winnicott and Bollas, among others, relational psychoanalysis further develops the notion of interpretation as a "complex relational event" (Mitchell, 1988, p. 295), emphasizing interpretation as an encounter that involves the transformation of both parties as they strive together for understanding within the context of their relationship.[1] For example, Aron (1996) critiques Bollas for not going far enough in acknowledging "the impact of the analyst's subjectivities on a patient or on the patient's subjectivity as a reflection of the impact of the analyst" (p. 86). He characterizes the analytic relationship as mutual, but because of the power differential inherent in the relationship, asymmetrical, and stresses the importance of analyzing "the patient's experience of the analyst's subjectivity" (p. 87). Aron maintains that the analyst's subjectivity is inherent in all interventions, including interpretations, and indeed, that this subjectivity is the very factor that makes them mutative. Acknowledging the impact of the analyst's subjectivity on the patient and of the patient's on the analyst frees both patient and analyst to engage differently, creating a space for the experience of new possibilities of relating that were previously unavailable.

Reminiscent of the Lurianic formulation of the contribution of the individual's divine spark that the soul brings to the interpretive encounter, Aron conceives of interpretation as emphasizing "the individual's unique, personal expressiveness" (p. 94). He says:

> I like to think of an analyst's interpretation as a creative expression of his or her conception of some aspect of the patient. Using the term this way, I believe that an analyst may interpret with a sense of conviction even while eschewing certainty and abandoning positivist epistemological presuppositions. (p. 94)

Interpretations are thus a function of the creative expression of the particular analyst in relationship with a particular patient at a particular time. In this view, the contribution to interpretation of the analyst's subjectivity is key. Interpretation is a reciprocal endeavor, a co-construction of meaning between both members of the dyad; relationship is the facilitative factor of transformation.

Mutual Transformation

Classical psychoanalysis traditionally conceived of transformation only in the patient, as facilitated by the analyst. From the perspective of relational psychoanalysis, transformation is no longer a one-way street but a two-party process. Although this idea did not achieve mainstream acceptance until relatively recently with the advent of the interpersonal school, even some early psychoanalytic thinkers (Ferenczi, 1932; Jung, 1929; Fromm, 1960, among others) insisted that the psychoanalytic encounter involved the mutual transformation of patient and analyst. As early as 1929, Jung wrote:

> For two personalities to meet is like mixing two different chemical substances: if there is any combination at all, both are transformed. In any effective psychological treatment the doctor is bound to influence the patient; but this influence can only take place if the patient has a reciprocal influence on the doctor. You

can exert no influence if you are not susceptible to influence. (Jung, 1929, p. 71)

Similarly, many contemporary psychoanalysts (Levenson, 1983; Gill, 1983; Mitchell, 1988; De Bianchedi, 1991; Wolstein, 1994; Aron, 1996, among others) argue that the analyst must be transformed by the encounter with the patient in order for mutative interpretation even to be possible. Following the interpersonal model, this is usually seen as experiencing and interacting within the particular relational matrix constituted by the analytic pair, getting caught up in it, and then working one's way out of it. Mitchell (1988) characterizes this "working one's way out" on the part of the analyst as:

the struggle ... to find an authentic voice in which to speak to the analysand, a voice more fully one's own, less shaped by the configurations and limited options of the analysand's relational matrix, and in so doing, offering the analysand a chance to broaden and expand the matrix. (p. 295)

Interpretation in this context is an attempt to "establish a boundary between the patient's experience and the analyst's and to bridge it simultaneously" (Schwartz, 1978, p. 9, cited in Mitchell, 1988, p. 296). Mitchell (1993) argues that, for analysis to be effective, both the analyst and the analysand must be passionate about the work. In his view, the analyst is not the purveyor of objective knowledge or merely a container within which the patient can find himself.

Rather, the greater the clarity, meaning, and enjoyment the analyst finds in his own participation, the better able he is to facilitate the patient's ability to expand her own experience while being able to enrich it in interactions with others. "What seems to me crucial in enabling the analyst to steer a course midway between claims to objectivity on the one hand and invisibility on the other is a love of the analytic inquiry itself and a deep appreciation of the awesome complexity of the human mind" (p. 84).

In his analysis of mutuality and asymmetry in the psychoanalytic dyad, Aron (1996) argues that mutuality "goes to the heart of the therapeutic relationship" (p. 126). This reciprocity also applies to interpretation, which rather than being administered by the analyst to the patient, occurs *in the space between* the patient and analyst, and has the potential of transforming either the patient or the analyst, or both. In other words, it is not a matter of being caught up only in the patient's psychic conflicts or ways of experiencing, but also in the analyst's. In relational psychoanalysis, Aron maintains, "neither pathology nor health is thought to reside in either the patient or the analyst exclusively, neither is the analyst thought to have a corner on truth and insight" (p. 127). Similarly, in her examination of Bion's formulation of mental growth, De Bianchedi (1991) concludes, "Psychoanalysis—or rather the psychoanalytic session as a privileged moment of inquisitive and reflective contact—can and should promote the tendency towards mental growth in *both members of the analytic couple*" (pp. 9–10).

What We Know

The term constructivism is increasingly used to characterize the epistemological paradigm shift currently taking place in contemporary psychoanalysis (Sorenson, 2004). Similar to the Lurianic formulation, constructivism stresses the unique spark of particularity that the knower brings to the interpretive encounter. Because "constructivism means there is more to knowing than knowing will ever know" (p. 57), a constructivist perspective implies that there is an element of faith inherent in all human knowledge. In the kabbalistic formulation, faith is central to knowing, and even more importantly, to becoming; it is its cornerstone. Faith encompasses and supports the kabbalist's willingness to remain in uncertainty, mystery, and doubt—his willingness to, momentarily at least, surrender the identity to which he normally clings in everyday life, in order to be at one with a greater reality. As Bion phrased it, the interpreter must "become infinite" (1977, p. 46) by relinquishing memory and desire, and to be patient, "'without irritable reaching after fact and reason' until a pattern 'evolves'" (1977, p. 124).

Although Bion was referring to the analyst, from a kabbalistic point of view, this applies equally as well to the patient. The patient, too, must be willing to have faith that something will evolve in the psychoanalysis, and must be prepared to remain in uncertainty, mystery, and doubt, painful as this state may be. The kabbalist is receptive to knowledge that cannot be attained via reason or objective observation, but can be encountered in at-one-ment with Ultimate Reality. In seeking truth, he understands the transformative necessity of losing his identity and being restored by finding his way back. So, too, the patient undergoing "catastrophic change" must shed her familiar identity in order to be open to transformative experience. The patient, like the analyst, must avoid using intellectual knowledge as a substitute for true transformation, or becoming, rather than mere knowing, which though necessary, is not sufficient. As I will elucidate in the next chapter, the kabbalists envisioned such creative transformation as entailing passage through no-thing, through the point of faith.

In the kabbalistic formulation, as in the relational psychoanalytic model, relationship facilitates transformation, and meaning is produced by the collaboration of both members of the interpretive pair. By perceiving their interpretive process as a dialogue with the divine, the kabbalists participated in what can be considered to be the archetypal paradigm of a mutual but most certainly asymmetrical relationship. After all, who possesses more power than God, who is the ultimate source of an infinite plenitude of meaning? But, despite their rejection of one truth or one correct meaning, the kabbalists did not reject the concept of truth itself in favor of a relative or narrative truth. They had faith in the existence of Absolute Truth, Ultimate Reality, the Godhead, O; they believed that the source of truth could be encountered within its infinite linguistic transformations.

Endnote

1. See Mitchell, 1988, and Aron, 1996, for a comprehensive treatment of this subject.

5. Faith as the Fulcrum
of Psychic Change

To a student who found himself tangled in doubts, Rabbi Baruch said, "You begin with a question and think, and think up an answer—and the first gate opens, and to a new question! And again you plumb it, find the solution, fling open the second gate—and look into a new question. On and on like this, deeper and deeper, until you have forced open the fiftieth gate. There you stare at a question whose answer no man has ever found, for if there were one who knew it, there would no longer be freedom of choice. But if you dare to probe still further, you plunge into the abyss."

"So I should go back all the way, to the very beginning?" cried the disciple.

"If you turn, you will not be going back," said Rabbi Baruch. "You will be standing beyond the last gate: you will stand in faith." (Buber, 1947, p. 92)

Although the role of faith in transformation is more frequently a topic of discussion in religious circles than in psychoanalytic ones, I contend that faith is pivotal to psychic change. Because the question of faith in the psychoanalytic literature is tackled from different, and often conflicting, perspectives, it is essential for me to define not only what I mean by faith, but also what I do not mean. By "faith," I do not mean religious faith, faith in an afterlife, or belief in God as an omniscient and omnipotent supernatural being directing the course of events in the natural world. Nor do I mean faith as some psychoanalytic writers (Isaacs, Alexander, and Haggard, 1963; Levin, 1998) have characterized it, as a state of mind that blocks perception of reality: as wish fulfillment, denial, or "unquestioning expectation of (magical) results" (Isaacs et al., 1963, p. 467). When I speak of faith, I am not speaking of an approach to life that advocates the abdication of personal responsibility, rejection of the freedom to choose, and submission of one's fate to an omnipotent authority, whether this authority be God or the analyst.

Rather, the faith I am referring to is in the unfolding potential that exists in the world at large and within one's self—what Ghent (1990) intuits as "the 'force' towards growth" (p. 110), the animating principle within us and beyond us that propels us toward self-understanding and self-expansion. Faith is our way of finding coherence in and giving meaning to the events and forces that shape our lives; it impels us to attempt to live our lives against a background of meaning and purpose (Fowler, 1981). In the context of self-transformation, including, but not limited to, psychoanalytic process, faith is a stance that is characterized by a willingness, for the sake of discovering one's authentic being, of finding one's emotional truth, to face that truth in all of its aspects: to plunge fully into the abyss of uncertainty and despair, to be open to what emerges, and so engage in an ongoing creative process of being and becoming (Eigen, 1981).

Faith comprises surrender. As Ghent (1990) notes, "Faith, surrender, the beginnings of creativity and symbol formation all intersect in the world of transitional experiencing" (p. 109). In faith, one fully experiences the present moment, letting go of defensive structures that include past and future, knowledge and certainty. Doing so entails tolerating anxiety and dread, even the terror of annihilation, which accompanies the shattering of defensive boundaries. Although, as in surrender, faith's "ultimate direction is the discovery of ... one's sense of self ... even one's sense of unity with other living beings" (p. 111), one does not know this for certain and cannot actively make it happen. Faith is not attained through certainty or willfulness but by surrendering to uncertainty.

The Paradox of Faith

Faith embodies paradox. In transformation, whether psychological or spiritual, faith entails standing still when one is consumed by the burning desire to move ahead. It asks of us to take a giant leap precisely at the times when we find ourselves most immobilized by fear. Although one may be desperate for answers, in faith one learns to "be patient toward all that is unsolved in your heart and ... try to love the questions themselves" (Rilke, 1934, p. 35). Faith and doubt exist side by side in continual tension (Sorenson, 2004), yet paradoxically, faith emerges not by resisting doubt but through embracing it. Only when we have questioned our most deeply held beliefs may we find ourselves standing in faith.

The story of Rabbi Baruch's student speaks to the limitations of reason and knowledge in facilitating self-understanding. When, like the student, we probe further and further with our intellect only to find ourselves tangled in doubts—in effect, rendered immobile by them—faith requires that we resist reaching for the lifeline of the known and familiar, and instead plunge headlong into the gaping void of uncertainty. The abyss of Rabbi Baruch's tale speaks to a particular mode of experience, alluded to by both poets and mystics. T. S. Eliot (1968) describes it as "the still point of the turning world" (p. 3); the Zen masters as the "'don't know' mind" (Epstein, 1996, p. 36); and the Kabbalah as no-thing, the void from which being emerges. Similarly, psychoanalytic formulations speak of remaining in the "nothingness which resides between the poles of paradoxical opposites" (Kumin, 1978, p. 482) and of maintaining "the tension between the need for discovery and the need for closure" (Ghent, 1992, p. 155). Standing in faith impels us to embody paradox: to leap beyond what is known into the void of the unknown, and at the same time, to experience the stillness of the present moment and to accept its truth.

This is by no means an easy task. Faith in the sense that I am using it here implies not an avoidance of accountability but, rather, its opposite—the willingness to take on one's life wholeheartedly, come what may. There is an active, animating quality to my characterization of faith, involving not only a receptive attentiveness to the "passionate longing to surrender" (Ghent, 1990, p. 115) but also an enflaming commitment and dedication to its realization. Fowler (1981) refers to this stance as a person's way of "moving into the force field of life" (p. 4). Eigen (1981), quoting the Shema, an ancient Jewish prayer, calls it "a way of experiencing which is undertaken with one's whole being, all out, 'with all one's heart, with all one's soul, and with all one's might'" (p. 413). Faith is our way of leaning into life.

Faith in the Psychoanalytic Relationship

Following Freud's (1927) characterization of religion and religious faith as wish fulfillment and illusion, classical psychoanalysis has traditionally distanced itself from an investigation of faith as an emotional state that facilitates cure. However, it is Freud (1914) who advocates a stance of faith (in the sense I am using it here) during the most intractable periods of analysis, highlighting the necessity of the analyst doing nothing but waiting, and simply allowing the psychoanalytic process to take its course. By doing so, he calls for an attitude of faith on the part of the analyst in the patient's ability to change, and in psychoanalysis as a vehicle of that change. As for the patient, Freud readily admits that "working through" is an "arduous task" and emphasizes that "it effects the greatest changes" (p. 154) and so the patient must be given the time to become "conversant" with his resistance and to work through it. The patient must come to fully experience in the present what was buried in the past, to accept that which she would rather deny, and to experience the disaffected material as emanating from her own being (Epstein, 1996). I suggest that the patient's willingness both to undertake and to tolerate this arduous task entails a stance of faith.

Much of the explicit conversation about faith (other than religious faith) in the psychoanalytic literature is one-sided, speaking only to and about the analyst.[1] Loewald (1960), for example, emphasizes the importance of the analyst's vision of the patient, of the analyst holding in safekeeping the image of the patient that will, in time, emerge into its own. Such a position implies that the analyst must have faith that the patient has the potential to be different from whom he is at the present moment. Most famously, faith plays a central role for Bion (1977b), who speaks of it as essential to the state of mind of the analyst, who must approach the analytic encounter free of memory and desire, having faith that each session has an emotional truth that will evolve if one is open to it. Contemporary psychoanalytic theorizing possesses the "inspirational aim of expanding and enriching human possibilities" (Summers, 2000, p. 547). The very nature of this aim requires the analyst's faith in these possibilities.

My goal in examining faith in a relational context is to shift the discussion of faith away from being grounded solely in the analyst's efforts to "cure" the patient, and to realign it as a mutual yet asymmetrical (Aron, 1996) stance on the part of both patient and analyst that is intrinsic to psychic change. The patient, not only the analyst, must at some crucial juncture stand in faith, in order for transformation to be possible. Like the analyst, the patient must be willing to shed the striving for mastery through reason in favor of the doubt and uncertainty that is prelude to being and becoming (Bion, 1977a). In the (asymmetrically) arduous task of transformation, it is the patient who must be able to plunge into the abyss that looms before her, to enter into the void that holds the potential for spiritual and psychic change.

As Safran (1999) has noted, the paradox of faith is built on the foundation of doubt and despair. For the patient, the leap into the abyss requires fully acknowledging and owning his feelings of hopelessness that things will ever be different. The analyst, too, must be able to stay in touch with her own experience of despair, to acknowledge the limitations inherent in helping another person and to recognize the associated feelings of hopelessness. At the point of faith, the patient as well as the analyst must be willing to "do" nothing, and simply "be," as painful as it might feel at the moment.

For psychoanalysis to be mutative, faith must bridge the psychoanalytic relationship. Through interactions with the analyst, in which old patterns of relating emerge and are transformed (Aron, 1991), the patient develops trust in the analyst as person and faith that a new way of relating is possible. This entails both subjective "being" on the part of each subject in the dyad as well as an intersubjective "being with" (Benjamin, 2004).

Within the stance of faith, "being" comprises the capacity to tolerate (at times painful) affect as well as ambivalence and conflict. It involves the ability to "become unintegrated, to flounder, to be in a state in which there is no orientation, to be able to exist for a time without being either a reactor to an external impingement or an active person with a direction of interest or movement" (Winnicott, 1958, p. 418). The capacity of the patient to "be" or, using Winnicott's terminology, to be alone in the presence of the analyst, is predicated on a relationship with a reliably present other who provides a safe holding environment. Notably, Slochower (1994, 1996) emphasizes the metaphoric holding of the analytic relationship in protecting the patient's subjectivity and at the same time facilitating the patient's movement toward object usage and mutuality. During the holding process, the patient is permitted his purely subjective experience without the impingement of the analyst's subjectivity, while the analyst struggles to retain (without expressing) "her capacity to imagine a movement toward an expanded analytic third" (Slochower, 1996, p. 327).

Benjamin (2004) formulates "being with" as a position of thirdness. The patient feels attuned to, recognized, "safely taken into the analyst's mind" (p. 28), while the analyst is able to remain empathically attuned to the patient and still maintain internal awareness. Benjamin links the capacity to "be with" the patient during the difficult times of analysis with the possibility of surrender. Through acknowledging her own vulnerability, even failure, the analyst is able to be receptive to the patient's catastrophic feelings and to bear them, while still maintaining her own sense of self. In turn, the patient, in sensing that his pain will not destroy the analyst, is able to experience feelings of terror and aloneness that were heretofore unbearable.

Bronheim (1994) notes that according to Jewish mystical tradition it is the honest examination of the truth about one's self within the context of relationship that is the leap of faith, the movement toward God. It is what compels Adam, after he has eaten from the Tree of Knowledge and attempted to hide himself from God, to respond to God's question, "Where are you?" by giving an honest account of his existential position—"I was afraid and I hid myself." Bronheim suggests that in psychoanalysis we too, continually ask our patients, "Where are you?" encouraging them to come out of hiding and reveal themselves, including exposing their "most intimate fears and feelings of shame when they admit 'I was afraid and I was hiding'" (p. 682). The very process of self-understanding requires that the patient take the leap of faith toward relationship. The analytic relationship of intersubjective recognition, of seeking out and finding, of being sought out and found, nurtures the emergence in the patient of a sense of identity and purpose. As she comes out of hiding, as she makes herself known and feels herself seen, the patient gradually formulates a meaningful answer to the question of where she is in the world.

As Bion's (1977a, b) vision of catastrophic change suggests, transformation of the psyche involves a continuous shattering and reorganization of previous and familiar ways of being, a falling apart and coming together. Through faith in 'O,' Bion writes, one becomes in touch with the catastrophic origins of the birth of one's psyche, the Beginning of existence that continues to inform the development of the self on an ongoing basis. Similarly, Mitchell (1993) speaks of the "constructive disintegration" of what is usually called regressive experience, "in which the ordinary contours of self experience become less guarded and more permeable, allowing an opening to and eventual integration of less controlled forms of experience not possible before, such as fusion and surrender" (p. 142). The analytic relationship provides a relational matrix within which disorganization and reorganization can safely take place. Winnicott (1954) locates in the chaos of regressive experience the hope for new opportunity for healing, as the false caretaker self is turned over to the analyst and the true self is allowed to emerge.

Psychic change, at the point of faith, entails a willingness to descend into fragmentation and chaos—to be shattered—so that one may reorganize into being capable of a richer, more fluid way of experiencing. The imagery of opposites—shattering and integration, no-thing and being, solitude and relationship, omnipotence and vulnerability—is used by the Kabbalah to portray the process of creative transformation, at whose fulcrum lies the paradox of faith. For a closer examination of the dimension of faith in psychic change, this chapter turns to these kabbalistic metaphors, specifically those of Creation and the ongoing creative process that, according to the Kabbalah, informs all existence. For the sake of clarity, I have chosen to omit some of the Kabbalah's more esoteric imagery as well as an exhaustive explanation of the sefirotic system, material that is readily available in the extensive body of work that comprises Kabbalah scholarship.[2] I choose instead to address those concepts that, in my view, most eloquently illuminate the role of faith in transformation.

Knowing and Being

How many of us have been asked by our patients (perhaps we have also asked ourselves) "I *know* this intellectually, but I don't *feel* it—what do I have to *do* in order to change?" In psychoanalytic circles, the issue has been framed as whether insight leads to cure or cure leads to insight. Ghent (1990) describes it as, "the schism between analysts whose emphasis is informational ... as against those whose focus is transformational" (p. 112). More cryptically, Bion refers to it as the problem of transformation in K (T→K) versus transformation in O (T→O), or knowing versus being.

The question of how one achieves self-understanding that leads not only to insight but also to meaningful change predates the psychoanalytic inquiry. In the 16th century, kabbalist Isaac Luria endeavored, in part, to answer this question by formulating a theory based on his original reading of the Zohar. Luria's theory of *tikkun* (restoration or repair) addresses the process of creative transformation on an individual and a cosmic level, proposing that each—the human being and God—is related to the other in an intimate relationship of mutual influence.

Whereas Bion (who frequently borrows his metaphors from the mystics) presents the issue of transformation in terms of "becoming 'O,'" or being at-one-with ultimate reality, the Kabbalah frames it as a question of *yesh meayin*, or how being emerges from no-thing. Like Bion, the Kabbalah differentiates understanding or knowing (T→K) from becoming (T→O), identifying faith as a stance that facilitates meaningful change. However, whereas Bion refers only to the state of mind of the analyst who is facilitating change in the patient, the Kabbalah insists that faith is intrinsic to self-understanding and ultimately to the process of transformation itself. In fact, according to the Kabbalah, without faith (i.e., on the part of the patient as well as the analyst), no change can occur at all. Most remarkably, the Kabbalah characterizes faith as a mutual yet asymmetrical stance, identifying it as the area of meeting between God and the human being. It refers to God's desire for relationship and mutual recognition and connection as a "divine leap of faith" and considers this encounter to be the highest developmental stage of both God and humanity.

The Divine Leap of Faith

Centuries before Winnicott conceived of potential space as a metaphorical area for creative experiencing on the individual and cultural level, this notion was central to the kabbalistic formulation of Creation on the cosmic level. Isaac Luria postulated that *Ein-sof* (the name for God meaning "without end" or "infinite") commenced the process of creation through an act of contraction, or *tzimtzum*, thereby forming a void pregnant with possibility—the primordial abyss. Into this space God revealed Himself through the emanation of the ten *sefirot*, or divine attributes, an interplay of dynamic potentialities and their relationships that permeate all planes of existence, including the physical world and the human psyche, and that change in every moment in a continual process of being and becoming.

In the Lurianic formulation, the *sefirot* are referred to as vessels, containers for the divine light. Not strong enough to contain it, the vessels shattered, and shards from the broken vessels fell, entrapping sparks of light in *klippot*, or husks, which became the basis of our world of material reality. Some of the light returned to its source, beginning the process of *tikkun olam*, restoration of the world, which continues through the restoration of the remaining light, trapped in *klippot*, to its source. *Tikkun* is accomplished through human acts, informed by intentionality, and through which the shattered fragments are reorganized into wholeness. Thus, both God and humanity are equal partners in an ongoing creative process that informs our world.

In its interpretation of Creation, the Zohar describes "a spark of impenetrable darkness" (*botsina de-qardinuta* in Aramaic; another translation is "spark that blinds") flashing within *Ein-sof*; Scholem (1995) terms this the "crisis" that turns *Ein-sof* from repose to creation. What spurred this crisis? According to the Zohar, it was the *ripple of desire for expression and manifestation* within the hidden recesses of the Infinite that caused *Ein-sof* to withdraw into Himself so that a finite world could be created. Quite remarkably, the Zohar attributes the motivation for Creation itself to *Ein-sof*'s desire for recognition by and connection with humanity—the desire to be perceived by His own creation and to enter into relationship with it. In turn, the individual seeks out God in relationship through his efforts to perceive the divine spark clothed within his own soul. This interplay of mutual recognition sustains the world, whose existence relies on the reciprocal flow of influence between the human and the divine.

In his formulation of surrender, Ghent (1990) suggests the existence of a force in the direction of growth "for which, interestingly, no satisfactory English word exists" and links it with a "longing to be known, recognized ... rooted in the primacy of object-seeking as a central motivational thrust in humans" (p. 110). The Zohar explicitly identifies this force as the primordial creative energy that animates all being, and posits that its source is the spark of God's "crisis"—His burning desire to be known by an Other.

This crisis or turning point of *Ein-sof*'s transformation from hiddenness to revelation is conceived as entailing passage through no-thing, or *ayin,* a formulation applied by the kabbalists to all transformation, including that of the human psyche. No-thingness is a liminal moment, "a stage of reality that lies between being wholly within the One and the first glimmer of separate existence" (Green, 2004, p. 38). The kabbalist Azriel interprets this crisis point between no-thing and being as the point of faith (Drob, 2000a). The startling conclusion reached by the kabbalists is that God's creation of the world, bringing it into being from the state of no-thing is, in essence, a divine leap of faith! Applying the kabbalistic principle of "as above, so below," faith is also seen as the locus of human creative and transformative activity, the point of no-thing from which being emerges.

The Sphere of Faith

The Kabbalah expresses God's progressive manifestation in terms of the *sefirot,* which are also seen as comprising the spheres of values and attributes of the human psyche. The *sefirot* are not meant to be a direct or complete representation of the Infinite, which is ultimately beyond the grasp of human perception. Rather, the kabbalists understand them as symbols through which the human psyche attempts to know itself and the world. The gap between human perception and the infinite and ineffable (Lacan's register of the Real or Bion's ultimate reality) is bridged, in the kabbalistic formulation, by faith.

The area of faith is represented in the sefirotic paradigm by the *sefira,* or attribute, of *chochma,* wisdom. In the sefirotic system, *chochma* is the link between the ineffable and the perceivable. *Chochma* emerges from the first *sefira, keter,* representing potentiality and desire, the aspect of God that is ineffable. Because it emerges from the unknowable and yet can be perceived by the human psyche, *chochma* is identified as *no-thing,* the liminal moment from which being emerges.

In the sefirotic tree, *chochma* is paired with the attribute of *bina,* or understanding, the ability to discriminate and to make distinctions. As we experience them as aspects of mind, *chochma* is the creative spark that is perceived as a flash of inspiration. *Bina* is the depth of thought that absorbs the spark, and refines, shapes, and articulates it, as a palace of mirrors infinitely reflects a spark of light (Green, 2004). From this pair emerges *daat,* knowledge. Here, the kabbalists formulate through the sefirotic vertex what Bion describes mathematically: being is not attained through knowledge (T→K) but emerges from the ineffable ultimate reality (T→O) in the sphere of faith (F).

Etymologically, *chochma* is comprised of *koach mah,* "the potentiality of what is" and *chakeh mah,* "wait—for what will come and what will be." Faith is a moment of pure receptivity where potentiality becomes manifest, in a flash of intuition that is wordless, but that seeks articulation. Standing in faith entails being open to "what will come and what will be" so that one may, for a moment, be at-one-with what is, with the divine spark that resides in one's soul. Although the source of our truth is ultimately unknowable, it is reflected in the palace of mirrors of our thoughts and actions, in a reverberating multiplicity of articulation and expression.

The Transcendent Third

Psychoanalysis has long grappled with the notion of the true self and the question of how it may be nurtured and actualized within the context of the psychoanalytic relationship. Are we a self or a multiplicity of selves? Is the true self already there and, if so, how can it be located? For Winnicott (1965), the true self is visible in the infant's spontaneous gesture and unfolds in relationship with its mother. In Loewald's model (1960), the parent holds a vision of the child's future that is "ideally, a more articulate and more integrated version of the core of being that the child presents to the parent" (p. 229). Greenberg (1996) writes that it is developed within the context of a deep and profound love. The mother who is empathically attuned to her child and at the same time aware of a future that the child cannot yet imagine is capable of "love that depends upon awareness and appreciation, in the moment, of actuality and potential, of the tension between the two, and of the possibilities for some resolution" (p. 892).

In the kabbalistic metaphor, the relationship within which one's truth is sought out and developed is not between two people, but between the individual and God, and so on the surface does not transfer easily into an application of technique in the psychoanalytic relationship. However, by bringing God into the equation, the kabbalists were free in a way that psychoanalysts have not traditionally been, to identify and articulate a dimension of psychological transformation that might best be described in terms of transcendent experience. The Kabbalah teaches us something new. Instead of reifying authenticity in terms of an essential true self or positing it as a social construction, the Kabbalah depicts it as a flicker of creative potential that lies within each of us and that resonates with, and is essential to, the larger creative energy that animates the world. In so doing, it emphasizes the singular value of a human life, the unique contribution of the individual to the larger whole, as expressed through the creative process of self-exploration.

Furthermore, it instructs us as to the ineffability of the human being, to our inability to know all that is to be known about another person, even about ourselves. Although we may reflect multiple facets, or experience a multiplicity of self-states, the truth of who we are is not contained in any one of them, but transcends them in a unity that remains beyond sensual perception. The uniqueness of the individual is elusive, requiring something other than reason or intellectual knowledge to discern it. Bollas (1987) notes the "mysterious unavailability of much of our knowledge" (p. 282), urging us to develop a relation to the unthought known within ourselves so that we may "address the mysteries of our existence" (pp. 282–283) and indeed, of existence itself.

It will be instructive at this point to highlight the Kabbalah's insistence that the sacred is to be found not in heaven but on earth. The Zohar is populated with wandering characters who come upon delights of concealed meaning in the course of their travels. In the Kabbalah, as might be said about psychoanalysis, the secret lies not at the end of the journey but rather in how one negotiates what is met on the way. En route, the traveler unexpectedly discovers the sacred within the ordinary, the meaningful within the mundane, the divine within the human. This theme lies at the heart of the kabbalistic view of transformation, and indeed, of life itself. If the kabbalist can be said to have a goal, it is to cultivate a refined perception capable of recognizing the sacred within the commonplace, and reciprocally, of infusing everyday acts with meaning, thereby elevating them to the level of the sacred.

In formulating psychic change in terms of the individual's relationship with God, the Kabbalah offers us a more expansive vertex from which to view the psychoanalytic undertaking. The kabbalistic model implies that the relationship between patient and analyst is deeply embedded in and facilitates the larger relational matrix that exists between the individual and the universal. It suggests that the psychoanalytic endeavor is imbued with a sacred significance—through the analytic relationship of intersubjective mutual recognition, in which we encounter ourselves in the heart of an empathic other, we at the same time approach God in relationship. Aron (2004) touches upon this idea when he writes, "As psychoanalysts, we should recognize that some of our cherished ideals are central to religious traditions and that in analyzing forms of aliveness and deadness, and thus in helping our patients to choose life, we are performing a sacred task" (p. 449).

In the meeting of minds of the analytic relationship (Aron, 1996) we open to the larger possibility of a mutual encounter with ultimate reality. In this potential space, which the Kabbalah characterizes as faith, we ask God the same question He asks of us, "Where are You?" and then we listen closely for the answer that whispers within us. We discover that we are held in the embrace of the ineffable and unknowable God who has been longing from the Beginning for this meeting to take place. We emerge transformed, having attained paradoxically, a sense of union with a larger whole and at the same time a heightened subjectivity, an expanded awareness of our individual identity that we may then purposefully, and with renewed energy, carry with us into our everyday lives.

In psychoanalytic terms, the analytic relationship is embedded in and potentiates a transcendent Third, a transformative area of experiencing that lies outside conscious will and yet is intrinsic to our human condition. The transcendent Third resonates with and enflames our inner-determined felt sense of authenticity; in this space, we are enlivened and (re)discover our unique meaning and purpose. I believe that this is what Benjamin (2004) means to describe in her formulation of thirdness as a relation to a "deeper law of reality" (p. 18). She writes that in this space, we transcend "the split between immersion and self-consciousness. ... That is where the Big Energy enters, in the open space of the third" (Benjamin, 2005, pp. 197–198). Drawing more explicitly from the kabbalistic metaphors, the transcendent Third is the point of faith, the area of encounter between the individual and God that facilitates the flow of divine plenty earthward, bringing both parties into balance.

Translated into the specifics of the psychoanalytic situation, the transcendent Third is potentiated by the relationship between patient and analyst, in which the patient's authenticity is given the opportunity to emerge within the framework of mutual, intersubjective recognition. Inevitably, there comes a crisis point, a moment in which it becomes frighteningly clear that there is a limit to what the analyst can do, and that the patient, and the patient alone, must take responsibility for his own life. At this crossroads, it is crucial for the analyst to be in touch with her own feelings of helplessness, to acknowledge her limitations in helping another person (Safran, 1999). She must not attempt to alleviate the patient's anxiety, nor her own, by offering reassurances that are not in her power to give and that would only be experienced as false hope.

This is the juncture where the patient finds himself on the brink, staring into the void. It is the point at which he must choose either to hang on to the dubious certainty that his defenses afford him or to let go, confronting the reality of his life such as it is. Here lies the opening of the transcendent Third. In choosing to leap into the abyss and to embrace the unknown, the patient allows the shattering of his defensive structures. He enters the potential space in which he encounters his own ineffable truth, experienced as a flash of inspiration, an ephemeral intuition, of the unique creative potential that lies within him, and of its relationship with the larger whole. He stands in faith.

The Spark That Blinds

The Kabbalah envisions the focal point of transformation as a "spark of impenetrable darkness" or "spark that blinds," a juncture that is the "point of faith." Interestingly, both Freud (cited in Bion, 1977b) and

Bion (1977b) use the identical metaphor in describing the analytic attitude required to perceive psychic phenomena, with Bion explicitly characterizing this attitude as one of faith:

> Freud said that he had to "blind myself artificially to focus all the light on one dark spot." This provides a useful formulation for describing the area I wish to cover by F. By rendering oneself "artificially blind" through the exclusion of memory and desire, one achieves F; the piercing shaft of darkness can be directed on the dark features of the analytic situation. Through F one can "see," "hear," and "feel" the mental phenomena of whose reality no practising psycho-analyst has any doubt though he cannot with any accuracy represent them by existing formulations. (p. 57)

Bion (1977b) insists on the necessity of the analyst maintaining a "state of naivety" (p. 159), and avoiding striving for knowledge. Resistance to transformation in "O" is manifest as a preference for knowing about something, rather than becoming it. Bion emphasizes that transformation in "O" is facilitated not through intellectual knowledge, which can get in the way of change, but rather through the willingness to tolerate *not knowing*, to stand in faith.

Similarly, from the kabbalistic perspective, reliance on the supports of reason alone is the "opposite of wisdom, and as such it cannot connect with the divine" (Steinsaltz, 2005, p. 129). Wisdom, or *chochma*, emerges in consciousness as a sense of truth that is beyond reason; at the point of faith, we cannot yet define it or explain why we feel it is true. Whereas Bion applies faith to the stance of the analyst in his perception of the emotional truth of a session, the Kabbalah's model suggests that the patient, too, must attain the "spark of impenetrable darkness," and stand in faith. Only when she has done so may she come in contact with the unique truth of herself, or her divine spark, her moment of at-onement with ultimate reality.

The Point of Meeting

The point of meeting between God and humanity is envisioned as a mutual embrace, a reciprocal reaching-out for connection from the world above and the world below, a connection that facilitates the flow of *shefa,* or divine plenitude. Freud might have called this the oceanic feeling; we might call the transcendent Third. While the Kabbalah accepts the gap between the ineffable and the perceivable, it maintains that encounter with God within the human psyche at the point of faith is not only possible, but even essential to sustaining the world.

Interestingly, Lacan (1977) proposes that a fundamental rupture from an original state of union characterizes the human condition, giving rise to desire that by its nature cannot be fulfilled. The Symbolic register is our attempt to represent this situation, which is beyond our grasp. According to Lacan, the register of the Real is lived experience of both the state of union and the rupture—experience that has been repressed and so remains outside awareness. Eigen (1981) identifies the creative play of meaning within the gap between one's self and the Other (the Unconscious, the Real, the Symbolic), as the area of faith:

> The subject's search for the truth about himself evolves by listening to a live play of meaning that always exceeds his grasp. Here faith is necessary. One cannot "master" the real, or life of meaning in any fundamental way. One can only try to participate in one's revisioning through impact and revelation, with all the openness and intensity of insight one can master. (p. 420)

In the kabbalistic view, the fundamental rupture, or *tzimtzum,* is a prerequisite for human existence, but it is a matter only of the necessary limitations of human perception. In order to live in the world, human consciousness experiences itself as separate. Yet because the human being is himself a manifestation of the divine, there exists the intimation of a greater oneness and the yearning for unity. The human desire for recognition and self-understanding is rooted in the longing of the divine spark to return to its source. The individual's movement toward the truth of herself enables her to create a life of meaning and is her unique contribution to Creation.

The paradox of Creation is that God's revelation occurs through an act of hiding, of cloaking the divine self in layers of garments so that God can be perceived by the human psyche, and can be desired, loved, and recognized. It is only through the emergence of a self-conscious "other," the human being who can both insist on the separateness of individual existence and at the same time acknowledge the Infinite, that the process of revelation meets its goal. Revelation is, in essence, relationship seeking, for the One who is revealed needs an Other to whom to be revealed (Green, 1993).

In the kabbalistic formulation, God seeks out human relationship in order to fully realize the potential of God's own growth and transformation, in other words, to be known. According to the Kabbalah, not only do human beings possess subjective self-consciousness, they were created with free will, the capacity to choose good as well as evil. As such, they pose a potential benefit as well as a serious risk to divine harmony and to creation itself. As God's partner in creation, humanity has the unique ability to affect the higher worlds through its actions in the lower world for better or worse, to perfect the divine relationships or to sever them.

Here we see another aspect of the divine leap of faith: *Ein-sof*'s movement toward vulnerability. The Kabbalah posits that *Ein-sof,* in effect, prefers the state of differentiation-in-relationship to the state of absolute-fullness-in-solitude, for the purpose of divine self-realization, despite the risks involved! Aron (2004) notes Jewish literature's portrayal of God as caring and compassionate, ambivalent and vulnerable, in His relationship with the human being. Eigen (1981) identifies this facet of self-other experience as "the area of faith" in his analysis of Winnicott's theory of object usage:

> The new awakening in object usage involves the realization that the other is in some basic way outside one's boundaries, is "wholly other." And while this may precipitate disorganization and dismay, it culminates in quickening and enhancing the subject's sense of aliveness. It opens the way for a new kind of freedom, one because there is radical otherness, a new realness of self-feeling exactly because the other is now felt as real as well. The core sense of creativeness that permeates transitional experiencing is reborn on a new level, in so far as genuine not-me nutriment becomes available for personal use. The subject can use otherness for true growth purposes, and, through the risk of difference as such, gains access to the genuinely new. (p. 415)

By choosing relation with the human "other" over remaining in omnipotent isolation, *Ein-sof* chooses "the risk of difference" for the purpose of divine growth. In making room for the "wholly other" He gains a partner who has the capacity to nourish His ongoing creative process, at the same time making Himself "vulnerable to the transformations genuine difference can bring" (p. 416). It must be emphasized that *Ein-sof* chose to create the human being with free will—in effect, to create a subject with his or her own "center of self" (Benjamin, 1990, p. 33) rather than a needs-fulfilling object—as His partner in relationship. In other words, *Ein-sof* chose vulnerability over omnipotence in order to participate in a mutually transformative relationship with humanity! Applied to the psychoanalytic endeavor, it underscores the relational understanding of the analytic relationship as a mutually transformative engagement, in which not only the patient but also the analyst, in allowing herself to be vulnerable, may "use" the other for her own emotional growth.

The Breaking of the Vessels

Imagery of shattering and containment, fragmentation and reorganization, destruction and restoration, permeates the kabbalistic formulation of primordial Creation and the ongoing creative process. It speaks to the inherent falling-apart and coming-together of change, to those times when familiar and understood structures can no longer stand, and existence as was previously known shatters into chaos. This chaos is the no-thingness of Creation, Rabbi Baruch's abyss, Bion's primordial catastrophe (Eigen, 1985). Chaos is the void of uncertainty that terrifies us; we unconsciously avoid it at all costs by seeking out containers for our anxieties and fears, finding dubious comfort in the known and the certain. Most terrifying of all, entering chaos means experiencing our own feelings of emptiness, abandonment, and despair, in all of their original and frightening intensity. Faith in the context of transformation involves not, as the traditional psychoanalytic view would have it, the creation of the illusion of security, but, rather, the shattering of it.

Bion associates the striving for knowledge (K) with the container-contained relationship, and faith with the analytic attitude that is open and receptive to emotional truth. However, particularly during the difficult times of an analysis, I believe that it is even more critical to speak of faith as essential to the attitude of the patient. As Ghent (1990) has emphasized, in order to change, it is the patient who must plunge into the abyss, and so shatter the security systems she has erected. The patient must suffer his own chaos and experience his painful feelings in the present moment. It is the patient, after all, who takes on the arduous task of psychic transformation. Nevertheless, the leap of faith on the part of the patient requires that both members of the analytic pair remain open to the possibility of surrender (Benjamin, 2004). In the analytic endeavor, "It is the process of breaking down and recreating that we commit to, itself a pattern or third that begins to unify the different, disparate moments. This process is the Big Energy in action" (Benjamin, 2005, p. 198).

In faith, the patient must be willing to tolerate emptiness and fragmentation until her own evolving truth reveals itself. Once this occurs, the flash of insight can be articulated and contained in the sphere of understanding, and fragmented shards of meaning can be restored and reorganized into new meaning. Emerging from chaos, the patient becomes attuned to a more fluid mode of experiencing, having gained the new understanding that chaos, although experienced as catastrophe, is not the equivalent of annihilation.

The Jewish mystical tradition makes a point of applying the metaphor of shattering and reorganization to attaining a higher spiritual rung. Interpreting a verse of the Zohar, the Hasidim of Kotzk make the paradoxical statement "There is nothing more whole than a broken heart." The intent of these phrases is to acknowledge the necessity of experiencing our pain, and to emphasize its value in our development. When we have experienced our own shattering, our heart broken into bits, it engenders in us an openness and sensitivity toward others, creating the possibility of true relationship; paradoxically, it enables us to fully experience joy. "Joy is experienced not necessarily as a consequence of crisis or as an opposite of sadness. Rather, it stems from an ability to arrive at an experience of truth" (Steinsaltz, 2005, p. 274).

A Case Example

I saw Ruth, a woman in her 50s, during my doctoral training. She grilled me about my qualifications, insisting that she needed a seasoned therapist, not a trainee. She would overwhelm me, as she had her previous therapists. She needed someone who could handle her.

Ruth was indeed overwhelming. During our first few weeks together, she presented with mysterious gynecological complaints that were medically unexplainable. In our weekly sessions, she described the inner workings of her body in minute and graphic detail. She spoke without pause, leaving no room for me to utter even a word. When I did try to speak, she simply talked over me with increasing intensity. At the end of each session, when I indicated it was time to stop, she continued speaking as if she hadn't heard me. I felt that in order to survive, I had to literally throw her out of the room: I would rise from my seat and open the door for her to leave, and yet her monologue continued to spill out into the hallway. I felt drained. I began to dread our appointments, in no small part because I could see no way of ending them tactfully.

During one of these sessions, Ruth complained at length that she was in excruciating pain. She believed that her doctors had not found its source because none had gone "deep enough" in examining her. What should she do? How could I help her? She paused for the first time, looking at me in desperation. I told her I could see that she was in great pain, but I did not have an answer. However, it occurred to me that perhaps she was also expressing a need to go deeper in therapy. Ruth replied that she had worn out her previous therapists until they had had enough of her. Although she had requested a second weekly session, each had rejected her, citing her history of frequently breaking appointments (as she also had done with me). If she could not make one appointment consistently, they would certainly not give her two. She had been afraid to ask me for a second session, knowing I would refuse.

I sensed at this moment that Ruth was telling me what she really needed, that she was offering me a foothold, a way to connect with her, which I had not yet been able to do. I had time in my schedule. I told her I would be willing to give her a second hour. Ruth's face lit up in an expression of genuine pleasure. She exclaimed, "You're a *guteh neshama!*" ("Good soul" in Yiddish) "I can see it in your face. Your face lights up the room." She was beaming. I could feel myself blush. Her response had taken me by surprise, and I was touched. Her tone and her words were familiar to me, felt as a faint glow of a loving childhood memory. My simple gesture of making room for her, of giving her the space to tell me all she needed to tell, had meant more to her than any of the few words I had managed to say during our previous sessions. It had signaled to her that however overwhelming she was, I was willing to be in the room with her and I would survive. In turn, she spontaneously let me know that she saw something new in me that she genuinely valued.

This was a turning point in our relationship, the moment in which each of us experienced the first glimmer of recognition in the other. In our following months together, little changed on the surface. Ruth continued to speak for the entire session and I continued to listen, rarely saying anything. But something had changed between us. She was no longer the oppressor and I the oppressed. Relinquishing my desire to speak, I surrendered to her need for me to simply listen. My surrender of the need to *do* something allowed me to *be with* her, and opened a space not available to us before. I found myself able to tell her of my dilemma in ending our sessions; she was able to suggest a way for me to get her attention, and to let her know when time was up.

Rather than feeling smothered by Ruth's words, I felt interested. Her somatic complaints gradually gave way to authentic expression of sadness and loss. At times, she displayed a disarming sense of humor that made me laugh. My laughter made her eyes twinkle, reflecting my recognition of an aspect of Ruth that had been hidden or lost. Slowly, I realized that I was seeing in my mind's eye not only the desperate, chronically ill woman sitting before me, but also the hopeful and vibrant young girl she had once been. Together, without my saying much of anything, we mourned the difference between the two.

Ruth had an effect on me even outside the therapy. I attended a formal dinner in the company of an elderly relative who often embarrassed me because he tended to be needy and demanding. On this occasion, although he had already received his meal, when he saw mine, he insisted that the waiter take his food back to the kitchen and bring him what I was having. Told there was none left, he began to argue and fuss in a way that normally would have infuriated and mortified me. Instead, I felt a surge of compassion. I cut my portion in two, and gave him half. His eyes lit up with gratitude. Later, I realized that my work with Ruth had transformed me. It had freed me to be generous in a way I had not previously been able.

Two months before my training year ended, Ruth began to panic. Her money was running out, she had no hope of finding a job, and I, the only person in the world who cared whether she was alive or dead, was leaving. I, too, felt panic, as well as guilt for leaving her. Unhelpfully, I pointed out to her that she had not actually been looking for work. She ignored me, listing all the reasons she would end up on the street, homeless, living in a box. Her anxiety increased. She cancelled sessions, unable to leave her apartment. She left messages saying she was spinning in the vortex of her own fear. She couldn't get out of bed, she hadn't showered, and she would only smell up my office if she came to see me. I didn't know what I could offer her, except to be with her. I called her and told her to come in anyway, that I was waiting.

She came in. She wore no makeup. Her hair was undone. She was clearly distraught, and yet she looked more real than I had ever seen her, and vulnerable. "I ran to you," she said. "It was either that or run out the window." For the first time, Ruth put into words what she had not previously been able to say. She admitted responsibility for the mistakes that had led to her current situation of lonely isolation. She acknowledged her defensive attempts to cover up and to appear more competent than she really was. She was furious that I was leaving and even more furious that she had deluded herself that I could somehow save her. Shouting, she cried, "I realize that I've been waiting all my life! I've been waiting for something to happen, for you to rescue me, for someone to hand me a job. I've been like a dead person. I can't wait anymore!" I listened, in the back of my mind applauding her strength in arriving at this painful insight, and at the same time wondering if she could handle it, or if she would threaten to kill herself and I would have to take her to the emergency room. In this moment, I envisioned her standing on the brink, neither of us knowing whether she would be able to take the leap and face her truths, or would back away from them, paralyzed by fear. Keenly aware of my own helplessness to help her, I felt myself in the presence of a decision being made, the cutting of a covenant between Ruth and God, as the two of them debated which way she should go.

In the following weeks, a change came over Ruth. She was calmer, more centered. Instead of trying to urgently convince me why she would never find a job, she began to look at employment ads and send out resumes. She bought an outfit that she could wear on interviews, and began speaking positively about her future. Much to my surprise, she began to speak enthusiastically about going back to school and pursuing the career that had been denied her as a young adult and that would allow her to make better use of her natural talents.

In our last session, Ruth gave me a gift, a necklace with a *hamsa,* a "hand of God" dangling from it. She told me that I would always have a place in her heart; in giving her a place in mine, I had touched her deeply. Although she knew she had more to work on, she had a renewed faith in her own resourcefulness. She would be able to do what she needed to take care of herself. I asked her how she had come to this place. Ruth replied that her gift to me symbolized her answer. After the session in which she arrived at her "moment of truth" in my office, she went home in a state of pure terror from which she was not sure she would emerge. Alone in her apartment, so anxious she was afraid to move from her position on her bed, Ruth fingered the pendant on her throat, a golden hand. Her mother had given her the necklace following the death of Ruth's baby, telling her, "I'm putting you in God's hands." Now, immersed in the depths of her despair, Ruth recalled her mother's words, and suddenly, she felt them to be true. She had a flash of intuition of her own resilience and resourcefulness, a realization that she experienced as a divine presence. Ruth told me that she could never have tolerated her despair had it not been for her therapy with me, in which I was a recognizing witness. Having been given the opportunity of our relationship, she said, she felt as though she had been held in God's hands.

Commentary

I purposely did not give the details of Ruth's life history and my formulation of her present difficulties, because for Ruth, it was not intellectual understanding, but the "being with" of our relationship that was so clearly the agent of change. From the initial glimmer of our mutual recognition, Ruth was able to take the leap of faith toward a relationship with me, and I toward her. In doing so, I found myself able to surrender to the immersion of empathic attunement while still holding on to my own sense of self. This created a space, or shared third, within which both of us could live.

As our relationship deepened, and a more authentic Ruth came into view, Ruth arrived at the edge of the abyss; the point where she realized that the defensive structures she had erected to protect herself had failed her. At that moment, Ruth had the choice of backing away from her anxiety and retreating once again into her defenses, or of entering fully into it and taking the leap of faith into the void. She chose to leap, experiencing her terror in all its catastrophic intensity. I could do nothing but be with her, the two of us standing together in the sphere of faith. Our stance was mutual, yet most certainly asymmetrical—although her relationship with me had facilitated this possibility, it was Ruth, not I, who was taking the plunge. Ultimately, Ruth's willingness to fully experience her despair enabled her surrender to the unknown, opening to the transcendent Third, an experience Ruth herself described as "being held in God's hands." Ruth emerged from this divine embrace transformed, having encountered within herself the creative life force that had been there all along.

Endnotes

1. An exception is Ghent (1990), who does not use the term faith but speaks to many of its aspects in his formulation of surrender.

2. See Scholem, 1969, 1987, 1991, 1995; Drob, 2000a, 2000b; Idel, 2002; Fine, 2003; Matt, 2004a, 2004b.

6. The Transformation of Evil

You are not obliged to finish the task, neither are you free to neglect it.

Pirkei Avot

This chapter addresses the problem of the transformation of evil, arguing for a moral imperative driving clinical work with patients who are traditionally considered untreatable. Psychoanalysts have historically been reluctant to make moral judgments; yet I propose that if psychoanalysis is to be relevant to contemporary human concerns, it must come to terms with the reality of human nature itself, namely its inherent potential for doing evil as well as good. In the words of Erich Fromm (1964), the unconscious:

> always represents the whole man, with all his potentialities for darkness and light; it always contains the basis for the different answer which man is capable of giving to the question which existence poses. ... The content of the unconscious, then, is not just the good or the evil, the rational or the irrational; it is both; it is all that is human. (p. 77)

Carrying the implication of moral condemnation and possessed of theological overtones, the term "evil" appears only rarely in the psychoanalytic literature as reference to a fact of worldly reality. It was not until 1930, when the implications of Germany's aspirations of an Aryan ideal became increasingly clear, that Freud (1930) directly addressed the "undeniable existence of evil" (p. 120), linking it explicitly to a destructive instinct in man. Having lived through one world war, and then, toward the end of his life, faced with the menace of Hitler, Freud was finally all too personally confronted with the chilling reality of evil. He ends *Civilization and its Discontents* by highlighting the precarious state of a world brought to the brink by man's destructiveness:

Men have gained control over the forces of nature to such an extent that with their help they would have no difficulty in exterminating one another to the last man. They know this, and hence comes a large part of their current unrest, their unhappiness and their mood of anxiety. And now it is to be expected the other of the two "Heavenly Powers," eternal Eros, will make an effort to assert himself in the struggle with his equally immortal adversary. But who can foresee with what success and with what result? (1930, p. 145)

Freud's evocation of the Heavenly Powers alludes to his recognition of the apocalyptic magnitude of the problem of good and evil, central to so much of religion and myth. Yet the psychoanalytic discourse following Freud rarely addresses evil as a fact of reality that must be acknowledged and dealt with in everyday life. Even Melanie Klein, who concerned herself so deeply with destructiveness and whose ideas are relevant to an understanding of evil, emphasized internal fantasy over outer reality.

Indeed, but for one recent exception (Grand, 2000), psychoanalysis appears to shy away from a direct in-depth clinical consideration of the problem of evil, preferring instead to leave it solely to the purview of religion and theology. It has been argued that because psychoanalysis is an empirical and observational scientific discipline, it should not venture to apply itself outside of its field of competence, including, specifically, the explication of evil (Bartolomei, Filippini, & Slotkin, 2001). Some psychoanalytic writers object to the use of the term altogether, arguing that calling something evil by definition places it outside the realm of comprehension. Twemlow (2000) writes, "the very idea of evil is beyond the pale of human understanding and thus beyond a possibility of resolution without divine intervention" (p. 776). Thinking deeply about the nature of evil is thus relegated to theologians, positioning it outside psychoanalytic discourse. A consequence of placing it beyond the sphere of human understanding is that it forecloses the possibility of effective human intervention. Driving the reluctance to examine evil from a psychoanalytic viewpoint is the notion that, while religion does not hesitate to make moral judgments, psychoanalysis should refrain from doing so.

Yet I believe that psychoanalytic judgments regarding evil *are* being made, albeit unconsciously and defensively. For psychoanalysts, "evil implies untreatability" (Winer, 2001, p. 619). The people who commit what we colloquially call evil—horrific or violent acts that deliberately cause suffering to other human beings—are often demonized. "They are particularly suitable scapegoats onto which we can project our own sadism" (Symington, 1980, p. 297). Few clinicians are willing to engage them in treatment. In our world post-9/11, terrorists and suicide bombers have shattered our presumptions of safety. Their monstrous acts, their apparent lack of conscience or guilt, their willingness to objectify their fellow human beings—these factors lead us to view these all-too-human perpetrators of evil as anything *but* human (Karen, 2003).

A review of the clinical literature suggests that we prefer to disassociate ourselves from evil, approaching it at a remove, most frequently in the form of literature or film analyses.[1] Our reluctance is understandable. Coming in contact with evil makes us vulnerable to being affected by it. It exposes us to the potential of malignant contagion, and forces us to face our own destructive possibilities. Instead of confronting evil directly, we recoil from its touch. We give it a poor prognosis for psychoanalytic treatment (Bird, 2001; Kernberg, 1971, 2006; Kernberg, 1996; Leahy, 1991), and choose not to undertake the task of its transformation. As any clinician who has recently worked within the organized mental health system must acknowledge, society reinforces our conviction that evildoers are untreatable; the only way to deal with them is to purge them from our midst, to lock the unrepentant in penitentiaries and to throw away the key—just as the ancient Israelites purged themselves of their communal sins on the Day of Atonement by sending a goat to Azazel, to wander in the wilderness and to be cast off the cliff (Leviticus 16:8).[2]

I do not presume to resolve the problem of evil, or to advance a solution in the form of the best psychoanalytic approach to treating evildoers. In fact, like most people, I would much prefer to leave evil alone, to avoid immersion in the gory details of the pain and misery human beings are capable of inflicting on one another. Yet to make the kabbalistic metaphors of transformation the focus of this book and to avoid the consideration of evil would be to omit the driving force, the moral imperative that informs this great body of thought, and its potential implications for clinical work. I propose that, as clinicians, we must acknowledge evil as a worldly reality if we are to truly contend with the human situation. Viktor Frankl (1984) has critiqued psychoanalysis for attending only to the individual's inner life, ignoring the importance of "man's search for meaning" which must be "discovered in the world rather than within man or his own psyche, as though it were a closed system" (p. 115). He writes:

> Ultimately, man should not ask what the meaning of his life is, but rather he must recognize that it is he who is asked. In a word, each man is questioned by life; and he can only answer to life by answering for his own life; to life he can only respond by being responsible. (pp. 113–114)

These are also the questions we must ask ourselves—what meaning informs our work as clinicians? Why do we do what we do and what do we hope to accomplish? If the aim of our work is repair and integration, can we in good conscience avoid dealing with evil and its repercussions? Is it all right for us to say that some people are worth treating and others are not? Can we afford to concede that the world is essentially unredeemable? Stern (2002) convincingly argues that although psychoanalysis has traditionally viewed itself as value-neutral, "there is another position, one that may have begun in the work of Erich Fromm and has been gaining adherents rapidly over the last two decades: psychoanalysis does not only investigate values, it promotes them" (p. 8).

Insisting that psychological reductionism is not sufficient to deal with the dilemmas of the human condition, Ernest Becker (1973) lauds

Fromm, calling him a "psychoanalytic prophet" for attempting to awaken a hopeful creative effort in humankind:

> Fromm has nicely argued ... that, as reality is partly the result of human effort, the person who prides himself on being a "hard-headed realist" and refrains from hopeful action is really abdicating the human task. This accent on human effort, vision, and hope in order to help shape reality seems to me largely to exonerate Fromm from the charges that he really is a "rabbi at heart" who is impelled to redeem man and cannot let the world be. If the alternative is fatalistic acceptance of the present human condition, then each of us is a rabbi—or had better be. (p. 278)

If, as Fromm envisioned, psychoanalysis encompasses hopeful human action, then it cannot in good conscience turn away from the totality of the human condition, including the reality of evil. But what is evil? Is it, as Freud suggested, a destructive instinct? Or is evil a relational event that might be transformed through the vehicle of the analytic relationship? Although religion and philosophy have long grappled with this question, psychoanalysis offers little in the way of explicit definitions of the nature of evil. This disparity in focus suggests that an investigation of evil from a more expansive perspective than that of psychoanalysis might be fruitful to contributing to the psychoanalytic understanding of it. Given its circumscribed field of inquiry, psychoanalysis might not be fully equipped to tackle the problem of evil; yet, given its concern with the life of the human individual, neither is it free to neglect it.

Seeing Evil

My goal in this chapter is to bring the discussion of evil into the domain of psychoanalytic discourse by examining the Kabbalah's ideas about evil through a psychoanalytic lens. In doing so, I hope to divest evil of its rarefied perception as a purely metaphysical problem that requires divine intervention for its resolution and to bring it down to earth, to the level of reality and hopeful human action. "Evil is there. What matters is how we meet it" (Clemmens, 1980, p. 291).

In contrast to psychoanalysis's tendency to "see no evil," as evidenced by its relative silence in the clinical literature, the Kabbalah acknowledges evil as an inevitability of worldly existence. Scholem (1969) explicitly characterizes 16th-century kabbalist Isaac Luria's theosophical system as a response to the expulsion of the Jews from Spain during the Inquisition, a period during which the evil inflicted on one human being by another (and in the name of God, at that!) reached catastrophic proportions.

On a fundamental level, the kabbalists grappled with the pressing problem of how to attribute meaning to existence in the face of the reality of evil. Their formulations can be characterized as pessimistically optimistic in the sense that, while they acknowledge the fact of evil and its destructive potential, they place the possibility of its transformation not in the hands of a transcendent God, but in the will and actions of the human being. Furthermore, by tying the unique intentions and acts of the individual to the rectification of the world, they ascribe a deep moral value to the human being's efforts to repair herself, to care for and cultivate the world in which she lives, and to perform acts of social justice even when confronted with injustice of catastrophic proportions. Although psychoanalysis has traditionally limited itself to the analysis of the inner life of the human being, the Kabbalah seeks to develop a wholling perspective that links the dynamics of a person's psyche with her external actions in the material world, including her relationship with others and the world at large.

Drawing on the kabbalistic metaphors, I discuss evil in terms of relationship and human free will, as capable of being transformed through the analytic relationship, rather than as the product of an inborn death instinct, which has been equated with the Christian theological formulation of original sin (Winnicott, 1971). Although I do not presume to arrive at the quintessential definition of evil, I wish to emphasize the realism, optimism, and the moral imperative inherent in the Kabbalah's principle of *tikkun*, and to suggest it as a model for informing the clinical work of psychoanalysis. I use the Zohar's commentary and Luria's metaphors to explore the Kabbalah's ideas about evil, and offer a clinical case to illustrate the way in which these ideas informed my work with a patient who exhibited antisocial traits and was considered untreatable.

The Roots of Evil

Although it is difficult if not impossible to reduce the Kabbalah's ideas about evil to a simple formula—several theories are advanced and exist side by side with one another—it will be instructive to return once again to the Zohar's formulation of Creation and Luria's notion of *tikkun*. The Zohar locates the roots of evil in *tzimtzum*, God's limitation of himself in making room for the world, humanity, and human free will. Using images such as shell, husk, and bark, the Zohar characterizes evil as the residue of Creation that fell to the *sitra achra*, or "other side," yet still encloses sparks of divine light. Luria uses similar imagery in his formulation of the *sefirot*, the divine values, as vessels, containers for the divine light. Not strong enough to contain the light, the vessels shattered, creating broken shards that tumbled through the void, entrapping sparks of light in husks, or *klippot*, that form the lower worlds, including the world of evil. Separated from its divine source, but still encapsulating light, evil is perpetuated and strengthened through human engagement. Some of the light returned to its source, beginning a process of *tikkun*, restoration or repair. Humanity's role in Creation is to continue the task of repairing the world through the restoration of the sparks to their divine source.

Evil is identified as a by-product of Creation, the broken shards of shattered vessels (values). Significantly—and here is the locus of the Kabbalah's optimism—evil still encapsulates light. The Kabbalah maintains that a spark of light exists within everything, including within Satan himself! The task of the human being in *tikkun* is to discern the divine sparks enclosed in their shards, and to elevate them, returning them to their source and bringing God Himself into balance. *Tikkun* is accomplished through humankind's moral, psychological, intellectual, and spiritual acts, including acts of social justice.

The transformation of evil via the restoration of the divine sparks is considered by the Kabbalah to be the ultimate meaning and purpose of humanity's existence, the central goal of the process of *tikkun*, and even the impetus behind the creation of a world that needs human beings to repair it (Steinsaltz, 1995). The highest moral and spiritual value is placed on human acts and intentions directed toward this end. Significantly, *tikkun* is not accomplished by intellectualization, by striving for transcendence, or by coming to some realization that our worldly identities or the world itself is illusory; it is done by engaging in the reality of the world as it is, with its inherent limitations, imperfections, and contradictions, and making the effort to improve it. Within this value system, the original perfection and self-sufficiency of Paradise is deemed to be less holy than an imperfect world elevated by human efforts.

Relevant to the psychoanalytic endeavor, the Kabbalah similarly values the imperfect individual who has made the effort to transform himself, to grapple with his own limitations, imperfections, and contradictions, and to improve upon them. The Kabbalah places the highest value on the individual's striving for *tikkun,* which it formulates as the unique contribution of the individual to the universal. Although it realistically acknowledges the difficulties inherent in this endeavor, pertinent to the psychoanalytic undertaking, it holds the *effort itself* in the highest esteem. According to the Kabbalah, more than the untouched goodness of one who has never come into contact with evil, God values the sweat and toil of the broken heart in its striving to become whole and approach God in relationship. This is the work of *teshuva,* or return, of the human being who has gone down into the depths, confronted evil, and transformed it by releasing the sparks of light contained within its husks. I suggest that this is also the moral imperative that drives our clinical efforts, and that informs the conviction that "mental health is not simply the capacity to love and to work. It is the struggle to behave with ethical strength on behalf of the other, and for oneself" (Grand, 2000, p. xi).

Turning away from Mutuality

In the Torah, the possibility of evil enters the field of human relations immediately after Creation, in the form of the snake. The snake is not in itself particularly dangerous if it is not approached. However, as the embodiment of evil, relationship with it is corrupting. Only humanity, created with consciousness and the freedom to choose, can "know" evil through relationally experiencing it. The snake urges Eve to eat from the Tree of Knowledge of Good and Evil, telling Eve that she and Adam will "be as God" if they do. Adam and Eve choose to eat the fruit, the only act God has forbidden them.

When confronted by God, Adam first blames God, "it was the woman *you gave me*" and then Eve, "she gave me of the tree and I ate it" (Genesis 3:12). Adam takes no responsibility for his action, disavowing the part of himself that transgressed God's command, and projecting it onto God and Eve. From a psychoanalytic point of view, evil's first manifestation in the interpersonal field is the individual's effort to rid himself of his own undesirable aspects and to transfer them via projection onto another. Goldman (1988) offers such an interpretation of the Genesis story, adding, "Evil ... involves a *move away* [italics mine] from the growth towards internal cohesion and wholeness that would be expressed by accepting and working towards integrating all aspects of one's being. ... It involves an effort ... to escape via projection from full knowledge of oneself" (p. 421).

The Jewish philosopher Martin Buber (1952) offers a similar definition of evil, identifying evil as the movement away from the personal wholeness that is necessary for true 'I-Thou' relation. For Buber, the "turning away" aspect of evil is twofold: it is the movement away from 'I-Thou' relationship with the other in the external world, from the point of meeting where mutual dialogue between two subjects is possible; and at the same time, a turning away from one's internal relation with the truth of one's being, from inner dialogue with one's divine spark of creative potential.

How different might Adam's relationship with God (and internally, with the truth of his own being) have been had he taken full responsibility for his actions? Instead, humanity is banished from the Garden and destined to embark on the road of struggle and suffering. Man must earn his bread through sweat and toil. He must undertake the hard labor of separating out the thorns and thistles from the herbs of the field for sustenance. Cherubim, angels wielding flaming swords, are placed at the entrance of the Garden, formidable obstacles standing in the way of humanity's return to Paradise.

The Zohar is fascinated by this story, offering numerous interpretations that reveal its ideas about the relationship between God and humanity and the role that human free will plays in the nurturance or severance of this relationship. Through hyperliteral interpretations of the text, the Zohar turns the tables on the traditional view of Adam as passively submitting to the seductions of the serpent and being put in his place by a vengeful God. Instead, it emphasizes Adam's autonomy,

maintaining that Adam chose to turn away from his mutual relationship with God and toward a non-mutual relationship with evil. The
Zohar portrays Adam as being curious about and delving into the dark
realms, thereby *arousing the snake to rise toward him*. Because Adam
reached down to evil, evil rose to meet him. Evil is stimulated by and
thrives only in its connection with human actions, taking its nourish-
ment from all that is good, yet annihilating it in the process. Bereft of
human engagement, evil would remain only a sterile possibility.

The Zohar emphasizes the relational consequences of Adam's
actions, including, rather remarkably, God's vulnerability in relationship with the human being. Adam's engagement with evil severs the
mutual relationship between Adam and God and also, as in Buber's
formulation, divides them each from themselves. In eating of the Tree
of Knowledge, the Zohar interprets, Adam severed the relationships
between God's *sefirot* or divine attributes, driving the *Shechina*, God's
feminine aspect, the aspect that is God's "I" or His immanence, out of
the Garden. According to this interpretation, it is Adam who installed
the Cherubim as barriers blocking his way back into the Garden. It was
not God's wish to do so. The *Shechina* is left abandoned and alone,
and humanity, too, is banished from Paradise. Together they wander in
exile, yearning to return to their proper contexts in relationship. As a
consequence of his engagement with evil, the human being has blocked
himself from the intimate and easy divine connection experienced in
Paradise. Further (and in the eyes of the kabbalists, this is one and the
same thing), he is exiled even from himself, cut off from effortless at-
one-ment with the divine spark of his creative potential.

On another level, because the human being has now absorbed
knowledge of good and evil (symbolized by eating the fruit), he must
discriminate and negotiate between them. Adam's lifelong task becomes
to till the soil of the earth to make his bread, to separate the thorns and
the thistles from the herbs that will nourish him. The Zohar interprets
these as hidden references to *tikkun;* the spiritual task of separating out
good from evil, gleaning the divine sparks from the husks that encompass them, thereby creating something new and life sustaining. Adam's
task, both literally and metaphorically, is the "cultivation of the world"
(Zohar 1:18a), which is "maintained through a rhythm of light and
darkness, good and evil. Human choice and action determine which
power will manifest on earth" (Matt, 2004a, p. 137).

Despite the seemingly disastrous consequences of Adam and Eve's actions, here again the Kabbalah is optimistic, suggesting that it was a necessary and positive step for both the world and humanity's development. In order to make his unique contribution to Creation, Adam has to exercise his freedom of choice. He has to "grow up" in order to deal with the more profound issues of life, to be engaged in the world in order to complete it. By exercising his free will, Adam severed his easy connection with God and so now must work to reconnect with God (and thereby with himself), and to improve the world he lives in. But something new is potentiated. Because of the struggle and toil required to perfect it, the world redeemed from evil is considered to be on a higher spiritual level even than Paradise, which needs no effort to be whole and complete.

Knowing Evil

In Hebrew, the word "to know" is used to mean knowing that is relational and experiential rather than intellectual and abstract. In knowing evil, the relational experience is not one of mutuality and intimacy; indeed it forecloses this possibility. The relational *modus operandi* of evil is that it lives off goodness at the same time it seeks to destroy it. As in Klein's (1957) characterization of envy as spoiling "the good object which is the source of life" (p. 189), the Zohar likens evil to a parasite that feeds off its host and by doing so, distorts and corrupts it.

Notably, Grand (2000) identifies the relational nexus of evil as the annihilation of the soul. She writes that the perpetrator's aim is to reduce "the victim to nothing but a body-it, devoid of freedom ... it extinguishes the victim's essential goodness, which the sadist envies and must destroy" (p. 90). It is only by feeding on goodness that evil has continued existence, as in the victim's bestial gesture of survival, in which "the perpetrator's guilt inhabits the survivor's soul" (p. 93). Furthermore, Grand describes the catastrophic loneliness experienced at the point of connection with evil, contending that it cannot be understood intellectually, only "known" relationally (Bromberg, 1994), language being a limited and insufficient medium with which to transform the experience of evil.

Hasidic thought (Buber, 1947; Steinsaltz, 1995) reads "knowledge" as the *relational experience* of good and evil internalized within the human psyche. The Hasidim are preoccupied with the turmoil that the ordinary person feels as a consequence of being pulled in two different directions, conceiving of the difference between good and evil not as a difference of quality, as in two different types of drives (such as Freud's *Eros* and *Thanatos*), but as "a difference of object" (Steinsaltz, 1988, p. 169). According to the Hasidic formulation, the inclination toward good or evil is the same, but one always has the possibility of changing one's direction. Because of the inherent difficulty in doing so, one who has most profoundly experienced a relationship with evil and transformed it toward the direction of a relationship with good is considered to be on a higher spiritual rung than one who has lived a saintly life. Changing one's direction in this way is conceived as *teshuva,* return, or turning toward God in relationship.

Repetition Compulsion as Tikkun

The Hasidic formulation evokes Fairbairn's (1946) understanding of libido as object seeking rather than pleasure seeking. Whereas Freud (1920) hypothesizes that the "compulsion to repeat" is the product of a death instinct that "is an urge inherent in organic life to restore an earlier state of things" (p. 36), Fairbairn reinterprets Freud's death instinct as relationships with internalized bad objects that are sadistic or masochistic in nature. He writes, "It is ... the nature of the object that determines the nature of the libidinal approach" (p. 31) and "for me, libido has direction" (p. 36). Furthermore, Fairbairn (1943) links his notion of the cathexis of bad and good objects with the individual's making a pact with the Devil, curable only by replacing it with a relationship with God, explicitly relating his formulation of libidinal 'badness' to the Hebraic conception of sin "as seeking after strange gods" (p. 74).

According to Fairbairn's model, the change in direction required for *teshuva* would be a particularly onerous and arduous task for one who has been passionately devoted to his repressed bad objects, as "the libidinal aim is in direct conflict with the therapeutic aim" (1943, p. 73), resulting in the negative therapeutic reaction. Similarly, the Hasidim recognize that the deeper one's involvement in a relationship with evil, the greater the obstacles in the path of return; thus the greater the value placed on the effort made by the individual to change direction.

Whereas Freud (1920) depicts the compulsion to repeat as hinting "of possession by some 'daemonic' power" (p. 36), the Kabbalah views it more optimistically, as a reparative striving. The Zohar refers to the soul being "rolled in the hollow of a sling," which Hasidic rabbi Schneuer Zalman of Liadi interprets as the soul confronting its failings during the course of its lifetime through remembering and reexperiencing past traumas (Steinsaltz, 2003). In what might be considered to be a Hasidic version of the repetition compulsion, Hasidic thought views the difficult circumstances in which a person repeatedly finds himself as opportunities for further sorting out and repair, offering him the possibility of rectifying himself and the world around him through his unique and individual acts of *tikkun*.

Likewise, Ghent (1990) discerns the reparative possibilities inherent in the compulsion to repeat, linking it with a striving toward growth. He attributes it to the wish to "take in," to understand, and to integrate past trauma, to reexperience that which was previously unthinkable, *for the sake of healing the self*. Repetition of destructive or self-destructive behavior, although painful, offers a "fresh opportunity for clarity ... rooted in a deep quest for understanding" (p. 127). Strikingly, Ghent characterizes sadistic and masochistic behavior as derivatives of "the wish to discover the reality of the other, and thereby truly experience the self." (p. 124). He writes:

> The pain and suffering of the masochist (and less obviously the sadist ...) may well be the excuse the caretaker self has devised to get the true self to where it has a chance of being found, a signal that something deep inside is rent, a tear in the self, that unbeknown to its bearer, seeks healing ... (p. 132)

In a similar vein, Tolpin (2002) emphasizes the reparative striving hidden within and yet made visible by the patient's pathology. She urges us to discern the fragments of health expressed by the patient's symptom, and to welcome and nurture them by interpreting them as such to the patient.

At heart, these formulations are optimistic about human possibility, yet realistic about human limitation. They characterize the difficult and often painful sorting out of the truth of one's self as the striving toward the direction of wholeness and mutuality in the service of healing and growth. From this vantage point of repetition compulsion as *tikkun,* or in Ghent's terms, repair of the rent in the self, the psychoanalytic task becomes to discern and to nurture the healthy striving toward healing that is both hidden in and expressed by the pathology. Here the Kabbalah's imagery of the divine spark "clothed" within the husk is a useful one, in that it captures the idea that something can be simultaneously hidden and made visible by that which hides it.

The Nature of Evil

According to the Zohar, moral evil involves separation and isolation, and the splitting of intimacy and mutual relationship into imbalance and exile. The person who enters into relationship with evil severs connection and is, on a deep level, exiled even from himself—from "what in his unique and non-repeatable created existence he is intended to be" (Buber, cited in Friedman, 2002, p. 120). Furthermore, evil involves grandiosity, the overstepping of boundaries, and the creation of false reality; it is characterized by hubris and self-inflation, presuming oneself, as in the snake's words, to "be as God." In the Zohar's formulation of evil, the attempt to take God's place is the opposite of faith, which is the point of meeting and mutual recognition between the human being and God.

The Zohar interprets Adam's choice as his attempt to push past the boundary of his human condition, to be equal to, or by defying Him, even to surpass God. By eating the forbidden fruit, Adam literally bites off more than he can chew, thereby giving evil a foothold in reality. Pushing past personal limitations for the sake of fulfilling one's creative potential is conceived as turning toward God in relationship. Knowing one's self deeply is formulated as the encounter with God in the sphere of faith. Presuming one's self to *be* God, however, is movement in the opposite direction, away from at-one-ment with the truth of one's being. The possibility of mutual, intersubjective relating is cut off, and the self exists in isolation, leading to destructiveness and the presumption of omnipotence.

Interestingly, Ghent (1990) explicitly roots the development of the destructive personality and its need for omnipotent control in what he calls the "failure of faith." Elaborating on Eigen's (1981) concept of the "area of faith" in the development of human consciousness and creative experiencing, Ghent identifies the "failure of faith" as the failure of the baby to transition from object relating to object usage, so necessary for the true self to come into being. When the caretaker fails the baby, that is, responds to the baby's natural and healthy destructiveness by retaliating or being destroyed, the baby is never able to discover the external reality of the other. The self develops in isolation, and the possibility of mutual, intersubjective relating is foreclosed. Further, the self comes to feel itself as actually destructive. In this isolated state, Ghent writes:

> fear and hatred of the other develops, and with them, characterological destructiveness comes into being. In short we have the setting for the development of sadism (in what remains a unit self, a self as isolate), the need to aggressively control the other as a perversion of object usage, much as we have seen in masochism as a perversion of surrender (p. 124).

The "failure of faith" severs real—enlivening and life-sustaining—connection. The other never breaks through the self's "destructive orbit" (Eigen, 1981, p. 417) of projections and introjections, and is never discovered as an autonomous subject. All that remains is self-created false reality, leading to real (rather than fantasized) destructiveness and the need for omnipotent control.

In her analysis of the perverse temptation, Chasseguet-Smirgel (1983) links perversion with man's desire "to go beyond the narrow limits of his condition ... one of the essential ways and means he applies in order to push forward the frontiers of what is possible and to unsettle reality" (p. 293). Perversion aims at subverting distinctions—upending law and destroying differences—with the goal of creating a new reality; thus Chasseguet-Smirgel characterizes perversion as "the equivalent of *Devil religion*" (p. 298). In perversion, she argues, one becomes God's rival, seeking to undo the separations, demarcations, distinctions, and naming that is Creation and to return to primal chaos. She concludes, "This reversal of a system of values is only the first stage in an operation whose end is the destruction of all values" (p. 299). Similar observations have been made about the psychopath, who is determined to attain his goals by "flouting the values which the society holds sacred" (Symington, 1980, p. 291).

I suggest that the destruction of values is not an end in itself, but at its root, a perverse attempt at healing, at seeking redemption, *but in the wrong direction*. Although Chasseguet-Smirgel contends that the pervert's objective is the destruction of reality and the reconstitution of chaos, she also maintains that the perverse desire to abolish difference is at the same time a response to and the denial of feelings of helplessness, distress, and dependence. "In fact, the abolition of differences prevents psychic suffering at all levels: feelings of inadequacy, castration, loss, absence, and death no longer exist" (p. 296). Following this line of thought, I would propose that the destruction of values is a perversion of the desire to push past one's limitations for the sake of growth, and is related to the longing for redemption, for the ushering in of a new order in which all suffering is relieved.

Transgression in the Service of Redemption

A vivid example of such 'transgression in the service of redemption' is provided in the history of the Kabbalah, in the person of the Shabbatai Zvi, born in 1626 in Smyrna, Turkey. By the time he was 18, the Shabbatai Zvi became a charismatic leader and developed a loyal following, teaching Kabbalah to groups of young men. Some kabbalists had predicted the coming of the Messiah in the year 1648; ironically, 1648 turned out to be a year of terrible suffering for the Jewish community in Eastern Europe at the hands of the Cossacks, with estimates of Jewish deaths running as high as 300,000.

The Shabbatai Zvi arose in the synagogue and pronounced God's name aloud, a heretical act, according to the Kabbalah, because he who pronounces God's name secures for himself power over the world. The rabbis of Smyrna pronounced a ban against him for his heresy. The Shabbatai Zvi declared himself the Messiah, cut up the parchment of the Torah and gave it to his followers to wear as shoes, then celebrated his marriage to the Torah in an elaborate ceremony. By cutting up the Torah and "marrying it," he sought to destroy the current social order and to usher in a new world order that would bring redemption. Through breaking the rules—literally, treading on them—he sought to transcend the suffering inherent in the human situation.

A heretical movement of nihilistic mysticism sprang from a radical wing of the Sabbatian movement. Scholem (1969) connects nihilistic mysticism with the symbol of Life that the mystic encounters in his mystical experience and that is associated with messianic freedom in redemption. In the nihilistic framework, Life is not harmonious relationship with God and submission to divine law but, rather, its opposite:

> Utterly free, fettered by no law or authority, this "Life" never ceases to produce forms and to destroy what it has produced. It is the anarchic promiscuity of all living things. Into this bubbling caldron, this continuum of destruction, the mystic plunges. To him it is the ultimate human experience. ... The nihilistic mystic descends into the abyss in which the freedom of living things is born; he passes through all the embodiments and forms that come his way, committing himself to none; and not content with rejecting and abrogating all values and laws, he tramples them underfoot and desecrates them, in order to attain the elixir of Life. (pp. 28–29)

Thus, the subversion of values can be considered to be a perversion of the desire for personal and universal redemption—as looking for relief from the turmoil and strife inherent in human existence, but in the wrong direction; or in biblical terms, as seeking after strange gods. Viewed in this way, evil is the malevolent miscarriage of human possibility, a consequence of grandiose denial of human limitations. Seeking to go beyond one's limits, or to envision a new world order, channeled toward the direction of goodness, as in a Gandhi or a Martin Luther King, is the noble and heroic manifestation of this desire; misdirected toward evil, this same passion has the potential of producing a self-appointed Messiah who sets out to redeem the world by destroying it.

According to Buber, radical evil manifests in the act of willful self-affirmation, which he equates with self-creation, the attempt to be God; it stands in opposition to the striving toward integrity and wholeness that is gained through authentic self-reflection (Friedman, 2002). Yet although radical evil takes on a substantive quality, it still has no absolute or independent existence—it is a matter of direction, a hardening within the individual against becoming what she was meant to be. In contrast, good is "the direction toward home" (p. 78); in Winnicott's terms, toward the emergence of the true self; in Bion's terms, toward the encounter with the truth of one's being; in the Kabbalah's terms, toward at-one-ment with the divine spark clothed within one's soul. Buber understands *teshuva* as response, in which the individual responds to the internal voice that calls on him to fulfill his unique creative potential. Such a response requires one to relate to this "other" of who one currently is, to listen attentively to one's emotional truth, and to answer to it.

Raising the Sparks

From a psychoanalytic point of view, this hardening or crystallization that so clearly and obviously stands in the way of the individual turning toward the good also opposes society's (and clinicians') willingness to view the evildoer as capable of change. Here, in both psychoanalytic and kabbalistic formulations of change, the key to *teshuva*, the point of turning, is discerning the spark that lies hidden within the husks. Melanie Klein expresses this notion:

> One of the great problems about criminals, which has always made them incomprehensible to the rest of the world, is their lack of natural human good feeling; but this lack is only apparent. When in analysis one reaches the deepest conflicts from which hate and anxiety spring, one also finds there the love as well. Love is not absent in the criminal, but it is hidden and buried in such a way that nothing but analysis can bring it to light. (cited in Symington, 1980, p. 294)

Both clinically and kabbalistically speaking, the task of transformation of even the most hardened criminal entails bringing to light the love that is buried within. Such an undertaking requires faith on the part of the analyst that even a person who appears to lack all human feeling is still, in fact, human. This is not to equate being human with being good but rather with the *possibility* of goodness. In order for the task of transformation to be undertaken in good faith, the clinician must operate under the assumption that the possibility of love exists. Furthermore, if the treatment is to carry any hope for redemption, the clinician must find within *herself* the possibility of love, compassion, or empathy for the individual who sits before her. In a fitting convergence of psychoanalytic and kabbalistic metaphors, the question of the transformation of evil becomes, "Will he or she let us into the living kernel from which true growth is possible—and are we up to the task?" (Ghent, 1990, p. 134).

We may not be able to accomplish that which we set out to do, despite our greatest efforts channeled in that direction. Thus the quote offered at the beginning of this chapter, "You are not obliged to complete the task, neither are you free to neglect it," urges a stance of pessimistic optimism. Although acknowledging the seeming impossibility of our clinical endeavors toward the transformation of evil, it speaks to the moral necessity of such an undertaking. If we believe that psychoanalysis is a "sacred task" (Aron, 2004, p. 449), we must put our faith not in God, nor in human nature, but in human possibility.

The Case of Stan

If you want to raise a man from mud and filth, do not think it is enough to keep standing on top and reaching down to him a helping hand. You must go all the way down yourself, down into mud and filth. Then take hold of him with strong hands and pull him and yourself out into the light.

Rabbi Shlomo of Karlin
(Buber, 1991, p. 277)

I saw Stan, a Jewish man in his 40s, while on an externship. My supervisor apologized for assigning him to me. She suspected he was a sociopath and that I would likely find him untreatable. A former drug dealer, Stan had a record of numerous robberies and assaults. He had threatened to kill his previous therapist at another facility, and had been banned by court order from returning. Stan was an imposing site. Tall and muscular, his body was covered with tattoos. A lightning bolt marked his shaved, bald head. Although physically and mentally able to work, Stan was actively manipulating the system, receiving welfare benefits after hiding his assets and declaring personal bankruptcy. He was applying for disability on psychological grounds, threatening that he would "lose it" (control of his anger) if his psychiatrist did not cooperate in filling out the paperwork. My supervisor told me there was only one good thing about him as a training case: "He comes."

She was right: Stan came on time for his initial session and for all of his subsequent sessions. He was narcissistic and grandiose, regaling me with tales of his glory days of drug dealing, when he had an abundance of power, money, and women. He bragged about ripping off the system: everybody else did—why shouldn't he? Being in the room with Stan felt to me as though I didn't exist for him at all. He rarely looked at me, and repeated the same stories using the identical phrasing, as if he had not told them to me before, or as if there were no one on the receiving end listening. I found myself fading into invisibility, my attention wandering. In supervision, I nicknamed him "Teflon man"—nothing I said, nor even my physical presence, seemed to stick. The same could be said about me. I had trouble remembering the content of our sessions, coming away from them with the feeling that they had been empty and that I had evaporated.

Maybe Stan *was* untreatable. He was convinced that "the system" was corrupt, and at times he almost succeeded in convincing me. He had made his drug connection through crooked cops; used the bankruptcy laws to stiff the credit card companies, large corporations who were ripping off the little guy with high interest rates; and was merely joining the swelling ranks of welfare scam artists to get what he felt was coming to him. Why should immigrants get a free ride while he was expected to work for a living? The unfairness of it all made him so angry he wanted to go out and smash someone with the baseball bat he kept in his car for just that purpose.

After attending the funeral of a colleague, Stan made a point of telling me that this man had suffered so excruciatingly from cancer that in death, his face had been frozen in an expression of torment. When I asked how he felt about this, hoping for a glimpse of compassion, Stan replied that he felt angry and ripped off: this man had used more than his share of Medicaid's resources. There would now be less left for him.

Stan certainly appeared to be a loveless and lawless sociopath. For all I knew, he was coming to treatment solely for the purpose of making a disability case. He had threatened to kill his previous therapist. Perhaps it was only a matter of time before he would "lose it" with me. But he did come consistently, and always on time, never even a minute late, a rarity in the facility in which I was working. I wondered if by being reliable, Stan might be taking me into consideration. Perhaps on some level he even valued our sessions.

As time went on, Stan began to acknowledge my presence in the room, albeit obliquely. He often made pop culture references from his youth, and although my responses clearly indicated that we were of the same generation and that I was familiar with them, inevitably he would say, "Of course you wouldn't know what I'm talking about—you're too young." I felt dismissed and oddly rejected, having been denied the opportunity to connect with him even on this superficial level. I wondered if by "young" he really meant "inexperienced," and therefore useless to him, which I was beginning to feel I was. But when I asked him what it meant to him, he replied, rather unexpectedly, that I was "too good" to understand how bad he really was. For the first time, he made direct eye contact. Having been brought out of my cloak of invisibility, I invited him to tell me what he sensed I thought of him. Again, his answer surprised me. He replied that I probably thought he was a loser. Whereas I clearly had my life together, his was a mess.

Gradually, Stan proceeded to let me in on just how bad he really was. He admitted to a feeling of bottomless emptiness, as if he had no center. If he could not be a drug dealer, he was nobody. His sex life had been reduced to masturbating to Internet porn. He had become obsessively preoccupied with downloading photographs of nude women, and cropping these pictures into body parts that he then enlarged and pasted together. Although he was ashamed of this, he could not stop himself. What woman would be interested in him now? Certainly not one who had her act together.

I took this as a reference to our relationship—would someone who was so "good" be interested in him, or had I written him off as a loser, as hopelessly untreatable? I suggested that perhaps his collages were an expression of his desire for a relationship that was greater than the sum of its parts—a more wholesome and meaningful relationship with a woman who would want to be with him, even without the money or drugs. Stan confessed that he had never believed this would be possible for him. His deepest fear was of being alone, and he was living it. He had no friends, no intimate relationships, and no hope of having a family. Experiencing these feelings made him want to beat someone up, which he might go and do after our session was over. He could find nothing about himself that was good, no aspect of himself that was redeemable.

Searching for any spark of light that I could authentically reflect back to him, I remembered my supervisor's words: "He comes." I pointed out to him that he was reliable. I could count on him to come, and I appreciated that about him. Where did that reliability come from? For the first time, Stan looked pleased. He told me that as a young adult he had had a construction business that he had prided himself on running well. He had given it up when offered a drug connection by a corrupt policeman, an offer he thought was too good to refuse. It would give him a chance to be somebody, unlike his father, who was weak-willed and powerless.

We began to explore his childhood, living in a disheveled home with a mentally ill mother and a passive but angry father, who would punch holes in the walls of their apartment rather than stand up for himself in a confrontation. Stan had felt ashamed of his mother and humiliated by and for his father, who was unable or unwilling to discipline his own son. Stan grew up in chaos. His parents set no limits on him, nor did they have any aspirations for him.

His maternal grandmother was the only person who fed him and cared for him during the frequent times that his mother was in a "state." Yet Stan repaid her kindness by stealing money from her purse. Although Stan's mother had been an unreliable caretaker, he had loved her. Yet he did not shed even a tear at her funeral, feeling no sadness, only anger at being "ripped off" by the nursing home that had put her in restraints and sedated her into a stupor. Most recently, Stan had burglarized the house of a man who had given him a second chance at a job, shooting his dog in the process. Possessed by an inexplicable fury, Stan finished off the burglary by flushing a wedding ring that had been lying on a dresser down the toilet. Stan could not say why he did it, but as we spoke, it became clear how envious he had been of this man's family life.

Although on the surface, he had "reformed" himself by being active in a recovery organization, Stan admitted to feeling like a fraud. Exhorting his sponsees to "bring God into your life," he felt hopeless of being able to do so himself. He had even tried to be "born again" by going to church with some recovery colleagues, but felt himself to be unredeemable. He had behaved so destructively toward others and had caused so much pain, why would God possibly be willing to come into his life?

I sensed that Stan was being more genuine with me at this moment than he had ever been in his adult life. Having shed his defensive grandiosity and pretense of omnipotence, he had exposed to me his shameful sense of inadequacy in its humiliating nakedness. Something had changed in me as well. I was able to emerge from my own state of dissociation, shaking off my cloak of invisibility and becoming newly present. I found that I cared about Stan. As he despaired, my heart went out to him. I said that as he had turned to Christianity in the hope of being redeemed, I wondered if he was aware of the principle in his own background, Judaism, that a person who had committed wrongful acts and repented was considered to be on a higher spiritual level than one who had only done good, because of the greater effort involved in turning one's self around.

At these words, Stan's demeanor noticeably shifted. His depressed mood seemed to lift. Perhaps he was feeling hopeful that he might actually be redeemable, or perhaps he only realized that I thought he was. He began to talk about the possibility of working and what jobs he might be able to do. He admitted to being ashamed of being on welfare. Thanks to the creativity of his psychiatrist, he had been approved for disability, but Stan now felt uncomfortable with the idea of taking it.

My time with Stan would end at the end of the training year. For several weeks, we talked about his feelings of being "ripped off": just when he had found a therapist he liked, it had to end. Because I was a trainee, he would not be able to continue seeing me. He was pissed off, angry; he thought he might "lose it." Finally, Stan missed an appointment. He did not return my phone calls, and I feared the worst—that he had indeed beaten someone up and landed in jail.

When Stan appeared for our next session, he told me what had happened. As he left his house the previous week, he found a truck blocking his driveway. The driver refused to move until he finished making the delivery. Furious, Stan took the baseball bat out of his car, getting ready to smash the windshield. A vision of my face appeared in his mind. He put it back in his car and called the police. When the police arrived, they told him he would have to wait until the driver finished. Stan was convinced they were corrupt and had been paid off. My face flew out of his head and he went around to the back of his car, took out the bat, and smashed the mirror of the police car. Stan spent the day in jail, missing his scheduled session with me. What had made Stan so angry in the first place? He was coming to see me and didn't want to be late.

For the next couple of weeks, Stan continued to be angry. He talked about being ripped off by the health care system, which was using trainees to make money for the hospital, without regard for the patients' needs. He was angry that I was leaving him and could not see him privately. In our last session, we talked about the possibility that he was sad: sad that he had had a relationship with someone he cared about and who cared about him, and that it was ending. He didn't think that was possible—he didn't have it in him. He had not even cried at his own mother's funeral. We said goodbye. As I rose to shake his hand, I noticed that his eyes were filled with tears.

Commentary

I chose the case of Stan because many considered him to be untreatable. One clinic even banned him from treatment via the justice system. Given his history, if I were in private practice rather than a trainee in a hospital, it is likely that I would have shunned him as well. Can Stan's actions be characterized as evil? I think so. He was violent and destructive toward others, and contemptuous of the laws and values of society, which he subverted and perverted toward his own ends. Stan wanted above all to "be somebody," and his attempts at self-cure included grandiosity, omnipotence, and sadistic violence. Yet underlying his repetitive destructive behavior was his longing to be redeemed from his deeply felt sense of inadequacy and shame, rooted in his childhood experience of being a nobody—of never having truly come into being. Stan's compulsion to rip off the system was fueled by his own sense of being ripped off: of being cheated of having a loving family in which he was a beloved and valued member. His pornographic collages and destruction of the wedding ring were symbolic of his desire for something more than his current isolation. They were distorted expressions of his authentic yearning for intimacy and relationship.

Detecting a spark of light in Stan was my attempt to find the possibility of goodness in him, and by doing so, to find compassion for him within myself, without which I could be of no help to him. I sensed that Stan's consistency and reliability in coming to our sessions were indications that he valued the possibility of a relationship with me, suggesting that on some level he had hope for himself. Reflecting back to him the possibility of his own goodness communicated to him that I had hope for him and for our work together. It gave him an inkling of his own creative potential, of a healthier direction he might take toward being somebody, a path that might lead to wholeness and mutual relationship, rather than the isolation and false reality of self-affirming grandiosity.

The "goodness" that Stan projected onto me in the transference that would stand in my way of understanding him reflected his dissociation from the possibility of his own goodness. Yet it also indicated that goodness existed as a possibility for Stan: he had a conscience that could discern the difference. In his linkage of my goodness with not knowing how bad he really was, Stan also detected an authentic aspect of our relationship. Given my own life experience, I could not really "know" (in the biblical sense) as he had, what it meant to be entangled in a relationship with evil. In fact, especially at the beginning of our treatment, I had a sense of being a "goody-two-shoes" sitting on the sidelines. It is likely that if we had more time together, Stan and I would have become involved in an enactment that would have allowed me to know his destructive potential (and possibly mine) more deeply.

Had Stan not explicitly brought up his longing for redemption in a relationship with God, I would not have mentioned to him the notion of *teshuva,* the effort to turn one's self around. Yet it still would have informed my work with him, as it enabled me to be pessimistically optimistic about the treatment. As his therapist, I truly appreciated the difficulty of his changing direction. In witnessing his emerging authenticity,

I had empathy for his struggle; and held the undertaking itself in the highest esteem.

Endnotes

1. See Bemporad, 2001; Cocks, 2003; Gottleib, 2000, among numerous others.

2. My experience on a psychiatric inpatient unit vividly corroborates this contention. A known sociopath was admitted to the unit and was immediately banned from all community meetings and from group and individual psycho-therapy. His "treatment" consisted of planning for his discharge starting from the day of his admission.

Epilogue
Jacob's Ladder

In the course of writing this book, I struggled with how best to present this material, as it is difficult to place a formal structure on concepts that can be so elusive and ephemeral. This is in fact why kabbalist Isaac Luria never wrote anything down, reportedly exclaiming, "When I open my mouth to speak, I find that everything is connected to everything else!" It is virtually impossible to offer a linear account, and therefore the reader may find that my exposition of kabbalistic concepts is more associative than linear in nature, similar to the style of the Kabbalah itself (but hopefully more accessible). My approach is layered, in that I show the different ways that the Kabbalah arrives at its conclusions—namely, through metaphor, symbolization (the *sefirotic* paradigm), and interpretation. I do so in order to convey the essence of the Kabbalah's complexity and creativity, characteristics that it might have in common with a well-conducted psychoanalysis.

In approaching Kabbalah, as I believe is also true of the psychoanalytic situation, one must begin with where one is, and trust that whatever path one chooses to follow will lead to where one needs to go. Understanding is attained not in a straight line but in an ever-deepening spiral; although we may sense that we have traveled a particular terrain before, each encounter with the material has the potential to reveal new meanings illuminated by shifting levels of awareness. I have by no means provided a complete explication of the Kabbalah's ideas, nor would I presume to be able to do so. In particular, I do not deal with kabbalistic meditative techniques or mystical praxis. The kabbalistic metaphors I have explored here are those that I believe are most relevant to the work of psychic change in psychoanalysis, and that have a particular resonance with the relational psychoanalytic paradigm. In elaborating on these metaphors and the Kabbalah's imagery of transformation in the context of relationship, I have attempted to give expression to what I perceive to be the ineffable aspects of the psychoanalytic encounter.

As I stated in the Introduction, my goal in this book is not to explain away spiritual experience in psychoanalytic terms, nor to suggest that we discard psychoanalytic formulations in favor of spiritual metaphors, but, rather, to play in the possibilities created by opening a dialogue between them. In considering our patients' experience—spiritual or otherwise—I believe that it is crucial to be keenly attentive to the ways in which our own subjectivities, including our relationship to theoretical models (whether they be psychoanalytic or theological or both), shape our understanding of what our patients bring to us, and equally as important, the questions we choose to ask of them, of ourselves, and of our profession as a whole.

Referring to awe, spirituality, and mystical experience, Ostow (2007) writes, "For reasons that I do not quite understand, accounts of experiences in the three categories considered here are seldom reported in psychotherapy or even in psychoanalysis." He concludes, "Perhaps the truly Spiritual life does not invite psychotherapy" (p. 47). If one takes into account the historical animosity between psychoanalysis and religion in general and psychoanalysts and religious belief in particular, this should come as no surprise. One may argue that in fact, it is the other way around—that because of its traditionally reductive interpretation of religious experience, psychoanalysis has not invited the truly Spiritual into the room. I strongly suspect that the frequency with which this type of experience is reported in psychoanalysis is directly related to the patient's perception of how the analyst is likely to perceive and interpret such experience.

In *Spirit, Mind, and Brain*, (2007) Ostow frames his central question as, "Is spiritual experience connected to something 'real,' in other words, a 'supernatural external influence,' or is it 'generated only by intrapsychic dynamics' and therefore an illusion?" (pp. 8–9) In accordance with the drive model, he concludes that the function of spiritual experience is illusory, serving to gratify the instinctual need for attachment. Ostow views awe, spirituality, and mystical experience as expressions of infantile longings, activated during periods of loneliness or depression. Using the language of classical psychoanalysis, he identifies the dynamics of mysticism as a "disturbance of the ego," a "regressive step backward, to hallucination and full loss of reality testing" (p. 45).

Ostow is primarily concerned with the distinction between reality and illusion, a concern that inevitably shapes his perspective. What is unfortunately lost in this focus and particularly in the use of such terms as "infantile" and "regressive step backwards" to describe the spiritual experience, is an appreciation of the transformative possibilities of illusion, the potential for enrichment and enlargement throughout the life cycle described so beautifully by Winnicott, Loewald, and others. As I have noted in the preceding chapters, contemporary psychoanalytic theorizing increasingly links illusion with imagination and vitality rather than with the satisfaction of drives and the avoidance of reality. In this view, one that I find particularly inspiring, "reality is encountered, inevitably, *through* imagination and fantasy. Fantasy and actuality are not alternatives; they interpenetrate and potentially enrich one another" (Mitchell, 2000, p. 84).

For Ostow, the unit of study is the individual. We are self-contained creatures, and our experience of connection with others is illusory. He writes:

Ultimately, of course, we are alone, confined within our bodies and the limitations of our minds. We entertain and encourage the illusion of "contact" with others. Our communication may include touch, speech, music, exchange of smiles and other facial expressions, exchange of gestures and actions, and exposure to the visible presence and the bodily warmth and scents of others. All of these create the illusion of contact, even union, not being alone. It is the illusion of lovers that their spirits are united; of the religious that they achieve some form of communication with God at some variable remove; of all of us that we are literal members of our community. But in fact, we live within the limits of our skin and our brains. A communication of minds, and metaphorically of hearts and souls, is illusory ... (p. 30)

For the kabbalists, the foreground and background are reversed, and it is our perception of boundary and separation that is illusory, although a necessary prerequisite for living in the material world of reality. Creation, both cosmic and personal, begins in primal unity and develops outward into complexity, toward the experience of individual identity and separate existence. The Kabbalah insists that the search for the other, the central motivational force that underlies human relatedness, is a microcosmic reflection of the life force that animates all being and that is the basis of all existence. Revelation requires encounter: the one who is revealed needs a recognizing other in order to fully come into being. In locating the divine within the human, and in placing relationship at the heart of the soul's fulfillment, the Kabbalah suggests that the point of meeting between self and other potentiates an experience of a deeper level of reality, of union and deep connection, in which God Himself is revealed.

In Genesis, we are told that Jacob dreams of a ladder, its base rooted solidly on the ground, its top reaching toward the heavens. On it, angels ascend and descend, moving heavenward from earth, and earthward from heaven. While Jacob dreams, God stands beside him. Jacob wakes from his dream and exclaims, "God is in this place, and I didn't realize it!" The Zohar interprets Jacob's ladder as the conduit through which the divine plenty flows, the channel of mutual influence that links the human and the divine, and which relies on relationship to remain open and sustain life. Furthermore, the Zohar identifies Jacob as the personification of this conduit. He represents the human capacity to move between different dimensions of being and levels of awareness. Significantly, God is encountered not in heaven, but on earth, standing right beside Jacob all along, longing to be recognized, and thereby revealed.

The imagery of Jacob's dream serves as a vivid illustration in spiritual terms of Loewald's psychological vision of "conscire," the "knowing together" of primary and secondary process that has been further developed by contemporary relational theorists (see Mitchell, 2000). In the relational framework, mind is comprised of a mutual relationship between different levels of mentation. Although primal unity is the original state from which consciousness emerges, it does not disappear, but continues to exist alongside higher modes of organization, serving as a source of renewal and vitality. In both the relational and kabbalistic paradigms, cultivating open channels between foreground and background, union and separateness, imagination and reality, makes the creation of new meaning possible, and potentiates the experience of the sacred.

References

Andresen, J. J. (1999). Awe and the transforming of awarenesses. Contemporary Psychoanalysis, 35: 507-521. [Note: awarenesses is correct]

Aron, L. (1990). One person and two person psychologies and the method of psychoanalysis. *Psychoanalytic Psychology,* 7: 475–485.

Aron, L. (1991). Working through the past—working toward the future. *Contemporary Psychoanalysis,* 27: 81–108.

Aron, L. (1996). *A Meeting of Minds: Mutuality in Psychoanalysis.* Hillsdale, NJ: The Analytic Press.

Aron, L. (2004). God's influence on my psychoanalytic vision and values. *Psychoanalytic Psychology,* 21: 442–451.

Aron, L. (2007). Black fire on white fire, resting on the knee of the Holy and Blessed One: Discussion of paper by Phillip Cushman. *Contemporary Psychoanalysis,* 1: 89–112.

Bakan, D. (1958). *Sigmund Freud and the Jewish mystical tradition.* New York: Schocken.

Bartolomei, G., Filippini, S., & Slotkin, P. (2001). Sadomasochistic perversion: object and theories. *International Journal of Psycho-Analysis,* 82: 1023–1027.

Becker, E. (1973). *The denial of death.* New York: The Free Press.

Bemporad, J. R. (2001). The complexity of evil. *Journal of the American Academy of Psychoanalysis,* 29: 147–171.

Benjamin, J. (1990). An outline of intersubjectivity. *Psychoanalytic Psychology,* 7: 33–46.

Benjamin, J. (1995). *Like subjects, love objects.* New Haven, CT: Yale University Press.

Benjamin, J. (2004). Beyond doer and done to: An intersubjective view of third-ness. *Psychoanalytic Quarterly, 74*: 5–46.

Benjamin, J. (2005). From many into one: Attention, energy, and the containing of multitudes. *Psychoanalytic Dialogues, 15*: 185–201.

Berg, P. S. (1988). *Kabbalah for the layman volume II*. New York: Research Center of Kabbalah Press.

Bettelheim, B. (1984). *Freud and man's soul*. New York: Vintage Books.

Biale, D. (1982). *Gershom Scholem, Kabbalah and counter-history*. Cambridge, MA: Harvard University Press.

Bion, W. R. (1977a). *Two papers: The grid and caesura*. Rio de Janeiro: Imago Editora.

Bion, W. R. (1977b). Transformations. In *Seven servants: Four works by Wilfred Bion*. New York: Aronson.

Bion, W. R. (1977c). Attention and interpretation. In *Seven servants: Four works by Wilfred Bion*. New York: Aronson.

Bion, W. R. (2005). *Cogitations*. London: Karnac Books.

Bird, H. R. (2001). Psychoanalytic perspectives on theories regarding the development of antisocial behavior. *Journal of the American Academy of Psychoanalysis, 29*: 57–71.

Bollas, C. (1987). *The shadow of the object*. New York: Columbia University Press.

Breuer, J., & Freud, S. (1893). Studies in hysteria. *Standard Edition, 2*: 1–305. London: Hogarth Press, 1955.

Bromberg, W. (1948). Dynamic aspects of psychopathic personality. *Psychoanalytic Quarterly, 17*: 58–70.

Bromberg, P. M. (1994). "Speak! That I may see you": Some reflections on dissociation, reality, and psychoanalytic listening. *Psychoanalytic Dialogues, 4*: 517-547.

Bronheim, H. E. (1994). Psychoanalysis and faith. *Journal of the American Academy of Psychoanalysis, 22*: 681–697.

Brown, L. S. (2007). The private practice of subversion: Psychology as tikkun olam. *American Psychologist, 52*: 449-462.

Buber, M. (1923). *I and Thou*, trans. W. Kaufman. New York: Charles Scribner's Sons, 1970.

Buber, M. (1947). *Tales of the Hasidim*, trans. O. Marx. New York: Schocken Books, 1991.

Buber, M. (1952). *Images of good and evil*, trans. M. Bullock. London: Routledge & Kegan Paul.

Buber, M. (1999). *Martin Buber on psychology and psychotherapy*, ed. J. B. Agassi. Syracuse, NY: Syracuse University Press.

Caplan, E. (1998). Popularizing American psychotherapy: The Emmanuel movement, 1906–1910. *History of Psychology, 1*: 289–314.

Chasseguet-Smirgel, J. (1983). Perversion and the universal law. *International Review of Psycho-Analysis, 10*: 293–301.

Clemmens, E. R. (1980). Good and evil—Reflections on the Parnas. *Journal of the American Academy of Psychoanalysis, 8*: 287–291.

Cocks, G. (2003). Stanley Kubrick's dream machine: Psychoanalysis, film, and history. *Annual of Psychoanalysis, 31*: 35–45.

Cushman, P. (1995). *Constructing the self, constructing America: A cultural history of psychotherapy.* New York: Da Capo Press.

Davidson, L. (2001). Idealization and reverence. *Journal of the American Academy of Psychoanalysis, 29*: 127–136.

De Bianchedi, E. T. (1991). Psychic change: The "becoming" of an inquiry. *International Journal of Psycho-Analysis, 2*: 6–15.

Diamond, S. A. (2003). Violence as secular evil: Forensic evaluation and treatment of violent offenders from the viewpoint of existential depth psychology. *Journal of Applied Psychoanalytic Studies, 5*: 21–45.

Drob, S. L. (2000a). *Kabbalistic metaphors: Jewish mystical themes in ancient and modern thought.* Northvale, NJ: Jason Aronson.

Drob, S. L. (2000b). *Symbols of the Kabbalah: Philosophical and psychological perspectives.* Northvale, NJ: Jason Aronson.

Eigen, M. (1981). The area of faith in Winnicott, Lacan, and Bion. *International Journal of Psycho-Analysis, 62*: 413–433.

Eigen, M. (1985). Toward Bion's starting point: Between catastrophe and faith. *International Journal of Psycho-Analysis, 66*: 321–330.

Eigen, M. (1998). *The psychoanalytic mystic.* New York: Free Association Books.

Einstein, A. (1993). *The world as I see it.* New York: Citadel Press.

Eliot, T. S. (1968). *Four quartets.* New York: Harcourt.

Epstein, M. (1996). *Thoughts without a thinker.* New York: Basic Books.

Ehrenberg, D. (1974). The intimate edge in therapeutic relatedness. *Contemporary Psychoanalysis, 10*, 423-437.

Fairbairn, W. R. D. (1946). Object-relationships and dynamic structure. *International Journal of Psycho-Analysis, 27*: 30–37.

Fairbairn, W. R. D. (1952). *Psychoanalytic studies of the personality.* London: Routledge & Kegan Paul.

Felstiner, J. (1995). *Paul Celan: Poet, survivor, Jew.* New Haven, CT: Yale University Press.

Ferenczi, S. (1932). *The clinical diary of Sandor Ferenczi,* ed. J. Dupont (trans. M. Balint & N.Z. Jackson). Cambridge, MA: Harvard University Press, 1988.

Fine, L. (2003). *Physician of the soul, healer of the cosmos: Isaac Luria and his kabbalistic fellowship.* Stanford, CA: Stanford University Press.

Fowler, J. W. (1981). *Stages of faith.* New York: HarperCollins Publishers.

Frankl, V. (1984). *Man's search for meaning.* New York: Simon and Schuster.

Frederickson, J. (2000). There's something "Youey" about you: The polyphonic unity of personhood. *Contemporary Psychoanalysis, 36*: 587–617.

Freud, S. (1894). Draft E: How anxiety originates. *Standard Edition, 1*: 189–195. London: Hogarth Press, 1966.

Freud, S. (1900). The interpretation of dreams. *Standard Edition, 4*: 1–338. London: Hogarth Press, 1953.

Freud, S. (1914). Remembering, repeating and working-through. *Standard Edition*, 12: 147–156. London: Hogarth Press, 1958.

Freud, S. (1920). Beyond the pleasure principle. *Standard Edition*, 18: 7–64. London: Hogarth Press, 1955.

Freud, S. (1927). The future of an illusion. *Standard Edition*, 21: 5–56. London: Hogarth Press, 1961.

Freud, S. (1930). Civilization and its discontents. *Standard Edition*, 21: 64–145. London: Hogarth Press, 1964.

Freud, S. (1933). New introductory lectures on psycho-analysis. *Standard Edition*, 20: 1–158. London: Hogarth Press, 1959.

Freud, S. (1937). Analysis terminable and interminable. *Standard Edition*, 23: 215–253. London: Hogarth Press, 1964.

Freud, S. (1940). An outline of psycho-analysis. *Standard Edition*, 23: 144–207. London: Hogarth Press, 1964.

Freud, S., & Abraham, K. (1965). *Letters, 1907–1926*, ed. H. C. Abraham & E. L. Freud. New York: Basic Books.

Friedman, M. S. (2002). *Martin Buber: The life of dialogue*. London: Routledge.

Fromm, E. (1960). Psychoanalysis and Zen Buddhism. In: *Zen Buddhism and Psychoanalysis*, ed. D.T. Suzuki, E. Fromm & R. DeMartino. New York: Harper & Row.   [**Author's note**: sorry I do not have the page ranges available]

Fromm, E. (1964). Humanism and psychoanalysis. *Contemporary Psychoanalysis*, 1: 69–79.

Fromm, E. (1994). *Escape from freedom*. New York: Holt.

Ghent, E. (1990). Masochism, submission, surrender—Masochism as a perversion of surrender. *Contemporary Psychoanalysis*, 26: 108–136.

Ghent, E. (1992). Paradox and process. *Psychoanalytic Dialogues*, 2: 135–159.

Ghent, E. (2002). Wish, need, drive. *Psychoanalytic Dialogues*, 12: 763–808.

Gill, M. M. (1983). The interpersonal paradigm and the degree of the therapist's involvement. *Contemporary Psychoanalysis*, 1, 200-237.

Goldman, H. A. (1988). Paradise destroyed: The crime of being born—A psychoanalytic study of the experience of evil. *Contemporary Psychoanalysis*, 24: 420–450.

Gottlieb, R. M. (2000). Hannibal. *Journal of the American Psychoanalytic Association*, 48: 1017–1019.

Grand, S. (2000). *The reproduction of evil*. Hillsdale, NJ: The Analytic Press.

Green, A. (1998). The primordial mind and the work of the negative. *International Journal of Psycho-Analysis*, 79: 649–665.

Green, A. (1999). *The work of the negative*. London: Free Association Books.

Green, A. (1993). *Seek my face: A Jewish mystical theology*. Woodstock, VT: Jewish Lights Publishing.

Green, A. (1999, September). A Kabbalah for the environmental age. *Tikkun Magazine*.

Green, A. (2004). *A guide to the Zohar*. Stanford, CA: Stanford University Press.

Greenberg, J. (1996). Loewald's transitional model. *Journal of the American Psychoanalytic Association*, 44, pp. 886–895.

Halperin, D. J. (1995). Methodological reflections on psychoanalysis and Judaic studies: a response to Mortimer Ostow (pp. 183-199). In: *Ultimate intimacy: The psychodynamics of Jewish mysticism*, ed. M. Ostow. London: Karnac Books.

Helem, L. (2004, July 12). The world on a string. *Newsweek*, p. 14.

Heschel, A. J. (1996). *Moral grandeur and spiritual audacity*. New York: Farrar, Straus, and Giroux.

Idel, M. (2002). *Absorbing perfections: Kabbalah and interpretation*. New Haven, CT: Yale University Press.

Isaacs, K. S., Alexander, J. M., & Haggard, E. A. (1963). Faith, trust and gullibility. *International Journal of Psycho-Analysis*, 44: 461–469.

James, W. (1902). *The Varieties of Religious Experience*. New York: Random House, 1999.

Jones, J. W. (2001). Hans Loewald: The psychoanalyst as mystic. *Psychoanalytic Review*, 88: 793–811.

Jones, J. W. (2002). *Terror and transformation*. New York: Taylor & Francis Inc.

Jung, C. G. (1929). *The practice of psychotherapy*, trans. R. F. C. Hull. Princeton, NJ: Princeton University Press, 1986.

Jung, C. G. (1963). *Mysterium coniunctionis: The collected works of C. G. Jung*, trans. R. F. C. Hull. Princeton, NJ: Princeton University Press.

Jung, C. G. (1963). *Letters*, Vol. 2. ed, G. Adler. Princeton, NJ: Princeton University Press, 1975.

Karen, R. (2003). Two faces of monotheism. *Contemporary Psychoanalysis*, 39: 637–663.

Kernberg, O. (2006, October). Transference focused psychotherapy. Presentation at Psychiatry Grand Rounds, North Shore University Hospital, Manhasset, NY.

Kernberg, O. F. (1971). Prognostic considerations regarding borderline personality organization. *Journal of the American Psychoanalytic Association*, 19: 595–635.

Kernberg, P. F. (1996, April). Clinical characteristics of antisocial children (pp. 1–19). Paper presented at the meeting of the International Psychoanalytical Association, Copenhagen, Denmark.

Klein, M. (1946). *Envy and gratitude and other works 1946–1963*, ed. M. Khan. London: Hogarth Press, 1975.

Kory, D. (2007, July/August). Psychologists aiding and abetting torture [Electronic version]. *Tikkun Magazine*.

Kumin, I. M. (1978). Developmental aspects of opposites and paradox. *International Review of Psychoanalysis*, 5: 477–484.

Lacan, J. (1977). *Ecrits: A selection*, trans. A. Sheridan. New York: Norton.

Leahy, M. M. (1991). Child sexual abuse: Origins, dynamics, and treatment. *Journal of the American Academy of Psychoanalysis*, 19: 385–395.

Levenson, E. A. (1983). *The ambiguity of change*. New York: Basic Books.

Levenson, E. A. (1988). The pursuit of the particular: On the psychoanalytic inquiry. *Contemporary Psychoanalysis*, 24: 1–16.

Levenson, E. A. (1995). A monopedal presentation of interpersonal psychoanalysis. *The Review of Interpersonal Psychoanalysis*, 1: 1–4.

Levin, R. (1998). Faith, paranoia, and trust in the psychoanalytic relationship. *Journal of the American Academy of Psychoanalysis*, 26: 553–572.

Loewald, H. W. (1960). On the therapeutic action of psycho-analysis. *International Journal of Psycho-Analysis*, 41: 16–33.

Loewald, H. (1978). *Psychoanalysis and the history of the individual*. New Haven, CT: Yale University Press.

Loewald, H. (1980). *Papers on psychoanalysis*. New Haven, CT: Yale University Press.

Lutzky, H. (1989). Reparation and tikkun: A comparison of the Kleinian and kabbalistic concepts. *International Review of Psycho-Analysis*, 16: 449–458.

Matt, D. C. (2004a). *The Zohar: Pritzker edition, volume I*. Stanford, CA: Stanford University Press.

Matt, D. C. (2004b). *The Zohar: Pritzker edition, volume II*. Stanford, CA: Stanford University Press.

McWilliams, N. (2004). *Psychoanalytic psychotherapy*. New York: Guilford Press.

Meissner, W. (1991). *What is effective in psychoanalytic theory: The move from interpretation to relation*. Northvale, NJ: Jason Aronson.

Meissner, W. W., & Schlauch, C. R. (2003). *Psyche and spirit: Dialectics of transformation*. Lanham, MD: University Press of America.

Meng, H., & Freud, E. L. (Eds.). (1963). *Psychoanalysis and faith: The letters of Sigmund Freud and Oskar Pfister*, trans. E. Mosbacher. New York: Basic Books.

Merkur, D. (1997). Freud and Hasidism. In: *Religion, society and psychoanalysis: Readings in contemporary theory*, ed. J. L. Jacobs & D. Capps. Boulder, CO: Westview Press.

Mitchel, S. A. (1988). *Relational concepts in psychoanalysis*. Cambridge, MA: Harvard University Press.

Mitchell, S. A. (1988). *Relational concepts in psychoanalysis*. Cambridge, MA: Harvard University Press.

Mitchell, S. A. (1993). *Hope and dread in psychoanalysis*. New York: Basic Books.

Mitchell, S. A. (2000). *Relationality*. Hillsdale, NJ: The Analytic Press.

Ogden, T. H. (1979). On projective identification. *International Journal of Psycho-Analysis*, 60: 357–373

Ostow, M., ed. (1995). *Ultimate intimacy: The psychodynamics of Jewish mysticism*. London: Karnac Books.

Ostow, M. (2007). *Spirit, mind, and brain: A psychoanalytic examination of spirituality and religion*. New York: Columbia University Press.

Philp, H. L. (1956). *Freud and religious belief*. London: Rockliff.

Pine, F. (1984). The interpretive moment: Variations on classical themes. *Bulletin of the Menninger Clinic,* 48: 54–71.

Rilke, R. M. (1934). *Letters to a young poet,* trans. M. D. Herter. New York: Norton, 1962.

Roazen, P. (1975). *Freud and his followers.* New York: Knopf.

Roback, A. A. (1957). *Freudiana.* Cambridge, MA: Sci-Art Publishers.

Rosenberg, D. (2000). *Dreams of being eaten alive: The literary core of the Kabbalah.* New York: Three Rivers Press.

Safran, J. D. (1999). Faith, despair, will, and the paradox of acceptance. *Contemporary Psychoanalysis,* 35: 5–23.

Salberg, J. (2007). Hidden in plain sight: Freud's Jewish identity revisited. *Psychoanalytic Dialogues,* 17: 197–217.

Scholem, G. (1969). *On the Kabbalah and its symbolism,* trans. R. Manheim. New York: Schocken Books.

Scholem, G. (1987). *Origins of the Kabbalah,* trans. R. J. Z. Werblowski. Princeton, NJ: Princeton University Press.

Scholem, G. (1991). *On the mystical shape of the Godhead,* trans. J. Neugroschel. New York: Schocken Books.

Scholem, G. (1995). *Major trends in Jewish mysticism.* New York: Schocken Books.

Schou, P. (2000). Future and potentiality in the psychoanalytic process. *Journal of the American Psychoanalytic Association,* 48: 759–783.

Simon, J. (1998, November). But all is not what it seems. *Self Magazine.*

Slochower, J. A. (1993). Mourning and the holding function of shiva. *Contemporary Psychoanalysis,* 29: 352–367.

Slochower, J. A. (1996). Holding and the fate of the analyst's subjectivity. *Psychoanalytic Dialogues,* 6: 323–353.

Sorenson, R. L. (1994). Ongoing change in psychoanalytic theory: Implications for analysis of religious experience. *Psychoanalytic Dialogues,* 4: 631–660.

Sorenson, R. (2004). *Minding spirituality.* New York: The Analytic Press.

Spezzano, C., & Gargiulo, G. J., eds. (1997). *Soul on the couch: Spirituality, religion, and morality in contemporary psychoanalysis.* Hillsdale, NJ: The Analytic Press.

Steinsaltz, A. (1980). *The thirteen petalled rose.* New York: Basic Books.

Steinsaltz, A. (1988). *The strife of the spirit.* Northvale, NJ: Aronson.

Steinsaltz, A. (1995). *In the beginning: Discourses on Hasidic thought.* Northvale, NJ: Aronson.

Steinsaltz, A. (2003). *Opening the Tanya: Discovering the moral and mystical teachings of a classic work of Kabbalah,* trans. Y. Tauber. San Francisco: Jossey-Bass.

Steinsaltz, A. (2005). *Learning from the Tanya.* San Francisco: Jossey-Bass.

Stern, D. B. (2002). A statement of mission. *Contemporary Psychoanalysis,* 38: 7–12.

Stern, T. (1996). Faith and denial. *Journal of the American Academy of Psychoanalysis,* 24: 545–554.

Sullivan, H. S. (1953). *The interpersonal theory of psychiatry*. New York: Norton.

Summers, F. (2000). The analyst's vision of the patient and therapeutic action. *Psychoanalytic Psychology, 17*: 547–564.

Symington, N. (1980). The response aroused by the psychopath. *International Review of Psychoanalysis, 7*: 291–298.

The truth about the Madonna cult. (2004, May 22). *The Daily Mail* (UK). Retrieved December 1, 2007, from http://www.rickross.com/reference/kabbalah/kabbalah65.html.

Tishby, I. (1994). *The wisdom of the Zohar*, volume III, trans. D. Goldstein. Oxford: The Littman Library of Jewish Civilization.

Tolpin, M. (2002). Chapter 11 Doing psychoanalysis of normal development: Forward edge transferences. *Progress in Self Psychology*. 18: 167-190

Twemlow, S. W. (2000). The roots of violence. *Psychoanalytic Quarterly, 69*: 741–785.

Weyand, C. E., ed. (1994). *Soul doctors: The first dictionary of psychology quotations*. Northridge, CA: Basic Books.

Winer, R. (2001). Evil in the mind of the therapist. *Contemporary Psychoanalysis, 37*: 613–622.

Winnicott, D. W. (1954). *Through paediatrics to psycho-analysis*. New York: Basic Books, 1975.

Winnicott, D. W. (1958). The capacity to be alone. *The International Journal of Psychoanalysis, 39*: 416–420.

Winnicott, D. W. (1960). The theory of the parent-infant relationship. *International Journal of Psychoanalysis, 41*: 585–595.

Winnicott, D. W. (1965). The maturational processes and the facilitating environment. *International Psychoanalytic Library, 64*: 1–276.

Winnicott, D. W. (1967). The location of cultural experience. *International Journal of Psychoanalysis, 48*: 368–372.

Winnicott, D. W. (1971). *Playing and reality*. New York: Basic Books.

Wolstein, B. (1994). The evolving newness of interpersonal psychoanalysis: From the vantage point of immediate experience. *Contemporary Psychoanalysis, 30*: 473-499.

Zornberg, A. G. (1995). *The beginning of desire: Reflections on Genesis*. New York: Doubleday.

Zornberg, A. G. (2002). *The particulars of rapture*. New York: Doubleday.

Index

A

Abraham
   change of name, 24
   and sacrifice of Issac, xi
Abyss, 63. *See also* Faith
   case example, 81–85
   necessity of leaping into, xx–xxi
   patient's need to plunge into, 67,
      76, 81
   psychic change as leap into, 28
Aggadah, 4
Analyst limitations, 76
Analyst subjectivity, inherence in all
      interventions, 57
Analytic relationship. *See also*
      Psychoanalytic dyad
   asymmetric nature of, 57
   metaphoric holding of, 68
   mutuality of, 57
   role in facilitating psychic change, 9
   shift in dynamic of, 27
   transformative nature of, 27
Aron, Lewis, ix, xxiii
Associative links, in kabbalistic
      thought, 54
Atonement, 27
Authenticity
   as flicker of creative potential, 74
   and transitional experiencing, 34

Awe, 27, 114, 115

B

Being
   and ability to tolerate pain,
      ambivalence, conflict, 67
   emergence from no-thing, 70
   vs. knowing, 53, 70
Being with, 68, 85
   as agent of change, 85–86
Bendel, 1
Berg, Philip, 1, 2
Book of Splendor, 45. *See also* Zohar
Buber, Martin, 14, 37, 45, 95
   knowledge of Hasidic tradition,
      14–15

C

Chabad, 2
   moral and ethical guidelines for
      living, 13
Chaim Vital, 17, 26, 52
Change of name, transformation and,
      23–24
Chariot mysticism *(merkavah),* 5
Chochma, 72
   as no-thing, 73

Christian Kabbalah, 19
Civilization and its Discontents, 88
Constructive disintegration, 69
Constructivism, 60
Cordovero, Moses, 5, 6
    Jung's appreciation of, 19
Creation
    as divine leap of faith, 72
    God's motivation for, 11, 71
    origin in primal unity, 116
    through act of contraction, 71
Creation metaphor, according to Luria,
    6
Creative potential, authenticity as
    flicker of, 74
Creative process, 80
    humanity and God as partners in, 4
    and longing for surrender, 32–37
    transformative possibilities of, 41
Creative transformation, 69
Cure, relationship with insight, 70

D

Desire
    analyst freedom of, 66
    beyond, 37–40
Dichotomization, critique of, xv
Direct divine communication, xii, xiii
Divine attributes *(sefirot),* 5
Divine embrace, 86
Divine plenitude *(shefa),* 78
Divine soul *(tzelem),* 14
    equation with personal authenticity,
    14
Divine sparks
    within evil, 93, 104–105
    in untreatable patients, 111
Divine vulnerability, 79
    in relationship with humans, 96
Dread, through abandonment of
    control, 40

E

Ein-sof, 71, 80
Einstein, on mystery, 31

Elijah, xvii
Evil
    in act of willful self-affirmation,
        103
    as attempt to be God, 103
    Buber's definition of, 95
    as by-product of creation, 93
    divine spark within, 104–105
    Freud's acknowledgment of, 88
    implication of untreatability, 89
    as inevitability of worldly existence,
        92
    kabbalistic ideas through
        psychoanalytic lens, 91
    knowing, 97–98
    knowledge of good and, 96
    nature of, 100–102
    as perverse attempt at healing, 102
    relegation to theology, 89
    and repetition compulsion, 98–100
    roots of, 93–94
    seeing, 91–92
    separation and isolation in, 100
    stan's case study, 105–110
    stimulation by human actions only,
        96
    transformation of, 87–91
    transformation through human will
        and actions, 92
    transformation via restoration of
        divine sparks, 93
    as transgression in service of
        redemption, 102–104
    as turn away from mutuality, 94–97
    as worldly reality, 90
Exile, through evil, 100

F

Faith
    case example, 81–85
    creation as divine leap of, 72
    divine leap of, 70, 71–72
    as essential to attitude of patient, 81
    evil and failure of, 101
    as force toward growth, 64
    as fulcrum of psychic change, 63–64

inherence in all human knowledge,
    60
leap of, 68
paradox of, 65–66
patient's stance in, 67, 68, 76, 86
in psychoanalytic relationship,
    66–69
role in transformation, 63
sphere of, 72–73
and surrender, 64
and transformation, xx
as unfolding potential, 64
False self, surrender of, 34
Fantasy-reality dyad, mutual
    interpenetration of, xvi
Flame imagery
    in divine encounter, 52
    predication on relationship, 55
Fragmentation, patient's need to
    tolerate, 81
Frankl, Viktor, 90
Free will, 79
    Adam's exercise of, 97
    in Genesis story, 95–96
Freud, Sigmund
    acknowledgment of evil, 88
    blending of rationality with
        subjectivity, xiv
    denial of Jewish origins of
        psychoanalysis, 17
    and goal of analysis, 22
    Hasidic books owned by, 18
    Hasidic descent of, 17
    ideas of religion and faith as wish
        fulfillment/illusion, 66
    identification as Jew, 17
    influence of Jewish mystical thought
        on, 16–19
    integration of scientific and sublime,
        28–32
    as last of the philosophers, xiv
    personal struggle for self-
        knowledge, 54
    self-characterization as rational
        atheist, 12
    self-distancing from traditional
        religion, 17

    treatment of creativity, discovery,
        and spirituality, 32
    view of intuition as illusion, 29

G

Gematria, 4, xix
Genesis story, 94, 95
    Zohar view of, 95–96
God's crisis, 72

H

Halevi, Yehuda, xiii
Hasidic tradition
    Buber's knowledge of, 14
    knowledge as relational experience
        of good and evil in, 98
    moral and ethical guidelines for
        living, 13
    mysticism as part of, xiii
Heavenly Voices, xvii
    lived experience of, ix–xiii
Holy of Holies, x, xi
Hubris, and development of evil, 100
Human condition, as rupture from
        original state of divine union,
        78
Human-divine partnership
    Jung's appreciation of, 19
    Luria's concept of, 6
    point of meeting, 77–80
    and transformation, 7
Humanity, as God's partner in
        creation, 79

I

Identity, transformative necessity of
        losing, 61
Illusion, 29
    of connection with others, 115
    separation and boundary as, 116
    spirituality as, 114–115
    as step towards relationship, 33
    as vehicle for attaining maturity, 33

In-between person *(beinoni)*, 13
Ineffability, 74
Insight, relationship with cure, 70
Interpretation
    as complex relational event, 57
    in context of relationship, 56–58
    as matter of mutual engagement, 51
    mutuality of, 52
    as one-way affair in classical
        psychoanalysis, 56
    process of, 49
    psychoanalytic, 54–56
    transformation through, 48–54,
        53, 56
Interpretive encounter, 45
    comparison to lovers' relationship,
        51
    and constructivism, 60–61
    in context of relationship, 56–58
    mutual arousal in, 51
    mutual transformation in, 58–60
    in psychoanalysis, 54–56
    and soul's journey, 45–46
    transformation through
        interpretation, 48–54
    transforming God through, 54
    and truth-seeking through
        language, 46–48
Intuition, as illusion per Freud, 29
Issac, sacrifice of, xi

J

Jacob, transformation through change
    of name, 24
Jacob's ladder, 113–117
James, William, 26–27, 31
Jewish Enlightenment, xiv
Jewish hermaneutical tradition, 11
Jewish law *(halacha)*, 4–5
Jewish mystical tradition
    influence on psychoanalytic theory,
        16–19
    Jung's appreciation of, 18–19
    psychoanalysis and, xiii
Journey of the soul, 45–46
Jung, Carl

critique by Buber, 15
    perception of links between Jewish
        mysticism and psychoanalytic
        theory, 18–19
    split with Freud over spirituality
        and mysticism, 27

K

Kabbalah
    as creative commentary, 4
    current popularization of, 2, 3
    and dual nature of human inquiry,
        12–15
    etymology of name, 2
    as fad, 1
    five elements of Jewish tradition in,
        4–5
    as hidden wisdom, 2
    historical context of scholarship,
        15–16
    infinite number of possible
        interpretations, 49
    link to Freud's ideas, 18
    medieval origins of, 3
    metaphors of transformation in, 10
    psychoanalysis and, 9–20
    rabbinic warnings on study of,
        xix–xx
    sexual metaphors in, 10
    shattering and containment
        imagery, 80–81
    16th-century revival in Safed, 5
Kabbalah Centres, 1
Knowing
    limitations in facilitating self-
        understanding, 65
    as relational and experiential, 97
    vs. becoming, 37–40
    vs. being, 53, 70

L

Language
    ability to capture experience
        through, xix
    creative and reparative powers of, 9

kabbalistic and psychoanalytic
    valuation of, 54
as medium of world creation, 4
of sefirotic symbolism, 48
symbology of consonants *vs.* letters
    in Torah, 50
as transformational vehicle, 22
truth-seeking through, 46–48
Libido, as object seeking, 98
Liturgy, and Kabbalah, 5
Loneliness, 101
in connection with evil, 97
in moral evil, 100
as ultimate reality, 115
in untreatable patients, 107, 108
Lubavitch Hasids, 2
Luria, Issac, 5, 6, 50–51, 52, 70, x
on interconnection, 113

M

Madonna
    "Die Another Day" video, 3
    self-proclamation as kabbalist, 1
Maimonides, 46
Meaning
    attributing in face of evil, 92
    man's search for, 90
    production through collaboration,
        61
Meister Eckhart, 19
Memory
    analyst freedom from, 66
    beyond, 37–40
Microcosm-macrocosm relationship,
    42
Midrashic sensitivity, 46–47
Mind, as embedded, 42
Minyan, xi
Moral judgments, reluctance of
    analysts to make, 87
Moses de Leon, 5, 45
Mother-infant relationship, 38
    and restoration of godhead, 40
    as root of sacred, 35–36
Mutual transformation, 58–60
    kabbalistic model of, 56

Mutuality
    evil as turning away from, 94–97
    spiritual perspective, 10
    in therapeutic relationship, 59
Mysticism
    Einstein on, 31
    and Jung's split with Freud, 27
    links to Rabbinic and Hasidic
        traditions, xiii
    and narcissism, 36
    nihilistic, 103
    split with rational religion, xiv

N

Narcissism, 36
Narrative tradition, and Kabbalah, 4
Nihilistic mysticism, 103
No-thing
    emergence of being from, 70
    wisdom as, 73
Not knowing, analyst's willingness to
    trust, 56

O

Object seeking, 98
Object usage, 79
Oceanic feeling
    as defensive/regressive phenomenon,
        30
    Freud's concept of, 29–30
Omnipotent isolation, 80
    presumption of, 100

P

Parapraxes, as symbolic events, 18
Play, of Torah's language, 49, 50
Point of meeting, 77–80
Prayer posture, early psychoanalytic
    understanding of, xv–xvii
Projective identification, 57
Prophecy, danger in eyes of Rabbinic
    tradition, xii
Psyche, 12

transformation of, 69
Psychic change
 as arduous task, 23
 faith as fulcrum of, 63–64
 as leap into abyss, 28
 role of analytic relationship in, 9
 through projective identification, 57
 and willingness to descend into
  fragmentation/chaos, 69
Psychoanalysis
 comparison with Zohar literary
  method, 46
 and dual nature of human inquiry,
  12
 as formulation of the godhead, 39
 historical animosity to spirituality,
  114
 and Jewish mystical tradition, xiii
 and Kabbalah, 9–20
 perception as value-neutral, 90
 permeable boundaries with religion,
  40–43
 reluctance to make moral
  judgments, 87
 as sacred task, 105
 shying away from clinical
  consideration of evil, 88
 spiritual and transformational
  aspects, 11
 and suppression of memory and
  desire, 39
 transformation as aim of, 21–23
Psychoanalytic dyad, 10
 actualization within context of, 73
 faith in, 66–69
Psychoanalytic interpretation, 54–56
Psychoanalytic theory, influence of
  Jewish mystical thought on,
  16–19
Public prayer, quorum for, xi

R

Rabbi Baruch, 80
Rabbi Bunam, 45
Rabbi Nachman of Bratzlav, 9
Rabbi Schneur Zalman of Liadi, 13, 14

Rabbi Shimon Bar Yochai, 45
Rabbi Zusya of Hanipol, 13
Rabbinic tradition
 conservative views of direct
  communications from God,
  xii
 of interpretation, xix
 mysticism as part of, xiii
Rational religion, split with irrational
  mysticism, xiv
Reason, limitations in facilitating self-
  understanding, 65
Red-string kabbalah bracelet, as
  celebrity fashion craze, 1
Regressive experience, 69
Relational psychoanalysis, 57
 intervention as two-party process
  in, 58
Relationship
 God's desire for, 70
 human ability to perfect divine, 54
 interpretation in context of, 46–48
 role in facilitating transformation,
  11
 seeking through revelation, 79
 symbiotic, 48
 and teshuva, 26
 water as metaphor for self-reflection
  in, 45
Religious experience
 historical animosity of
  psychoanalysis to, 114
 permeable boundaries with
  psychoanalysis, 40–43
 transformation in, 23–25
Repair of the world (tikkun olam), 2,
  5, 6
 as journey toward self-realization,
  11
Repentance
 spiritual growth inherent in, 109
 transformation through, 25
Repetition compulsion, as tikkun,
  98–100
Resistance, 66
Revelation, as relationship seeking, 79
Reverence, 27

S

Sacredness
within the commonplace, 75
on earth, 74
in psychoanalytic endeavor, 75
Safed
kabbalists of, 5
as site of kabbalistic revival, 5
Scholem, Gershom, 15–16
Sefer Yetzirah, 5
Sefirot, 5, 12, 57, 93
as aspects of God clothed in
garments, 48
God's progressive manifestation in
terms of, 72
as vessels for divine light, 71
Sexuality, kabbalistic and
psychoanalytic concepts of,
18
Shabbatai Zvi, 102–103
Shattering/containment imagery, 80
and attainment of higher spiritual
rung, 81
Shefa, 78
Snake, corrupting relationship with, 94
Sociopaths, 105–110
Soul essence, as being *vs.* knowing,
53, 55
Spirituality, 115
early psychoanalytic understandings
of, xv–xvi
historical animosity between
psychoanalysis and, 114
as illusion *vs.* reality, 114–115
Striving, high kabbalistic value on, 94
Surrender, 27, 65, 72
faith and, 64
longing for, 32–37, 34
and transformation, 35
Symbiotic relationship, 48
Symbols, in Kabbalah, 54

T

Tanya, 13, 14
Teshuva, 25, 94, 98, 104, 111
as point of turning, 104

and relationship, 26
Therapeutic relationship. *See also*
Analytic relationship
mutuality and asymmetry in, 59
Tikkun olam, 2, 6, 71
Jewish law practice and, 5
as journey toward self-realization,
11
and mutually sustaining divine-
human relationship, 53
and reparation, 10
repetition compulsion as, 98–100
value of individual striving for, 94
Torah, as plaything bestowed by God,
49
Transcendent third, 73–76, 86
Transference-countertransference, 111
transformative possibilities of, 41
Transformation, 21, 69, xvi, xvii
and aims of analysis, 21–23
beyond memory and desire, 37–40
and change of name/place, 23–24,
25
and creativity, 32–37
of evil, 87–91
and Freud's integration of scientific
and sublime, 28–32
of God himself, 55
in hardened criminals, 104
infant experience of mother as
process of, 35
integrating perspectives of, 26–28
Kabbalah's metaphors of, 10
kabbalistic example of, 25–26
and leap into abyss, xx–xxi
and longing for surrender, 32–37
mutual, 55, 58–60
ongoing nature through
psychoanalysis, 23
psychoanalytic *vs.* Hasidic views
of, xx
in religious experience, 23–25
and renewal, 32–37
role of faith in, 63
role of relationship in facilitating,
11
as spark that blinds, 76–77
through divine embrace, 86

through interpretation, 48–54
through repentance, 25
transformation possibilities of, 34
Transgression, in service of
    redemption, 102–104
Transitional experiencing, creativity
    and religious feeling as, 33
Truth, 48
    symbology of Hebrew consonants
    in, 47
Tzimtzum, 30, 93

U

Untreatable patients, 92, 110
    case study, 105–110
    evil and, 87

V

Vulnerability, divine, 79

W

Wailing Wall, x. *See also* Western Wall
    of Jerusalem
Water
    continuous mutability of, 56
    as metaphor for self-reflection in
    relationship, 45, 56
Western Wall of Jerusalem, ix–xiii, xv,
    xvii
Wisdom *(chochma)*, 72
    as no-thing, 73
    as sense of truth beyond reason, 77
Working through, 66

Z

Zohar, 1, 5, 26, 45, 48
    concepts of evil, 93
    definitions of evil, 95
    literary method of, 46